# Riding *on* Rainbows

## Blackpool Pleasure Beach and its Place in British Popular Culture

John K. Walton

SKELTER
PUBLISHING

First published in 2007 by
Skelter Publishing LLP
3 Connaught Road
St Albans
Herts
AL3 5RX

www.skelterpublishing.com



A catalogue record for this book is available from the British Library

ISBN 978-0-9544573-6-5

Designed and typeset in Great Britain by Paul Barrett Book Production, Cambridge.
Printed by Piggott Black Bear, Cambridge

# Contents

# About John Walton

John K. Walton is Professor of Social History at the University of Central Lancashire. From November 2007 he will be Professor of Social History in the Institute for Northern Studies at Leeds Metropolitan University. He has worked on the history of the British seaside (especially Blackpool and Whitby) for many years, as well as writing about tourism and resorts in Spain (especially San Sebastián), Belgium, France, the United States (especially Coney Island), and Latin America. He also writes about popular culture, regional history and regional identities, especially in Lancashire and the Basque Country. His books include The Blackpool landlady (Manchester, 1978); The English seaside resort 1750–1914 (Leicester, 1983); Lancashire: a social history 1558–1939 (Manchester, 1987); Fish and chips and the British working class, 1870–1940 (Leicester, 1992); Blackpool (Edinburgh, 1998); The British seaside: holidays and resorts in the twentieth century (Manchester, 2000); and (with Gary Cross), The playful crowd: pleasure places in the twentieth century (New York, 2005).

# Preface

This book is a cultural and social history of Blackpool Pleasure Beach. It makes extensive use of the Pleasure Beach's own archives, and I acknowledge the help, expertise and advice of Ted Lightbown with gratitude. But it is neither an official nor a commissioned history, and it seeks to provide an outsider's view of the Pleasure Beach's development and significance. The company has had no direct input into content or interpretation. Nor can it be an economic or business history, as no access has been sought to the financial and management archives of this private limited company. It looks at who experienced the Pleasure Beach and its rides, and what they said about it, and it sets the fortunes of the amusement park in the context of developments in Blackpool and the wider world. It owes a considerable debt to those amusement park enthusiasts who have compiled careful and often scholarly archives of their own, and made them accessible through websites. It also owes a great deal to colleagues in the Department of Humanities at the University of Central Lancashire; to Dr Vanessa Toulmin of the National Fairground Archive at the University of Sheffield; and to my grandparents, Solomon and Elsie Walton, who retired in the mid-1960s to Arlington Avenue, two streets away from the Pleasure Beach, and helped to stimulate my early interest in it. Above all, the book's completion has been made easier and more enjoyable by my new domestic working environment in the centre of Lancaster, and by the moral support provided by Gillian, the best wife a man could wish for, and by my wonderful step-daughters Christine and Lydia.

*Lancaster, 5 November 2006.*

# 1 Blackpool and the Pleasure Beach

Blackpool Pleasure Beach is Britain's most popular tourist attraction. Its website lays claim to over 6.2 million visitors in 2005, and the town's local authority, which put the figure at an even more impressive 7 million (a reminder that the statistics are somewhat 'soft'), claimed that it was the second most popular amusement park in Europe and the ninth in the world.[1] Official figures from VisitBritain were only slightly less bullish, putting the Pleasure Beach at 6 million visitors during 2004–5.[2] Its 42 acres contain 145 'rides, attractions and shows', including ten coasters, and there are 45 cafes and restaurants. It beat the 'high culture' attractions of the National Gallery and British Museum comfortably into second and third place, one and a half million visitors behind. It left rival amusement parks trailing far in its wake, as well as the revitalised surviving Brighton Pier that soared into fourth place in 2004–5, and its comfortable ascendancy over the metropolitan museums led the *Guardian* to comment rather condescendingly that, 'If the hurtling rides and candy floss of that excellent but intellectually undemanding resort are so closely tailed by Raphael and the Rosetta Stone, we need hardly fear for the cultural well-being of the nation.'[3] But the Pleasure Beach defies condescension, and it is not necessarily 'intellectually undemanding'. It has continued to invest and innovate into the twenty-first century, with four major new rides (Valhalla, the Spin Doctor, Bling and Infusion) coming on stream since 2000, while a new generation of management has taken the amusement park's tradition of family ownership into a fourth generation and a new century.[4] The Pleasure Beach's own website emphasizes its identification with family values, both in the sense that it seeks to cater comfortably for families, and in the sense that it has always been family run and can trace a genealogy back to a founding father, William George Bean, at the turn of the nineteenth and twentieth centuries. Bean himself is credited with a defining expression of the Pleasure Beach's purpose in the website's presentation of its history: 'We wanted an American Style Amusement Park... to make adults feel like children again

1 www.blackpoolpleasurebeach.com/HTML/index.php accessed 3 January 2006; www.business.blackpool.gov.uk/sections/secret/pb.aspx accessed 3 January 2006.

2 *Guardian*, 5 Aug. 2006, p. 6.

3 *Guardian*, 21 Feb. 2005, p. 17.

4 www.aboutbritain.com/BlackpoolPleasureBeach.htm accessed 6 January 2006.

and to inspire gaiety of a primarily innocent character.'[5] It is a spectacular national and international phenomenon, and it deserves the serious attention of historians. We need to ask why it has been so successful, over such a long period, while rival seaside amusement parks have faltered and fallen by the wayside; to ask what this success means, and what it suggests about continuities and changes in British popular culture over the last hectic century; and to explore the potential tensions between the Pleasure Beach's identities as business, purveyor of thrills and excitement, and embodiment of family values, and see how they have been resolved in practice.

The Pleasure Beach's capacity for attracting the crowds, keeping their loyalty and broadening its appeal has deep roots in British popular culture. Within a few years of the first raucous stirrings of machinery and mirth on the sand dunes of Blackpool's South Shore at the beginning of the twentieth century, this pioneer among British amusement parks was already famous, first across a wide area of northern England, then across the nation and beyond. It was an exciting illustration, at once stimulating and disturbing, of the spending power and capacity for noisy, cheerful, collective enjoyment that came to be displayed by a new generation of industrial workers in the late nineteenth and early twentieth century. But it began life as a place of entertainment for adults, and children were not much in evidence until the boom in working-class family holidaymaking in the expansive years after the Second World War, when paid holidays became general and spending power increased enough to enable poorer families with young children (as opposed to younger people without responsibilities, and older families with teenagers at work) to enjoy a few cheap days at the seaside for the first time.[6]

At the turn of the nineteenth and twentieth centuries the working classes of the Lancashire 'cotton towns', in particular, were benefiting from falling prices, steady employment, unusually high family incomes (fuelled by the waged work of women and teenagers, and based on a trade-off between time and money that produced a high-pressure lifestyle of working hard and playing hard in limited free time), and the capacity to save while they spent, especially at favourable points in the life cycle. From this relatively prosperous environment (compared with earlier years and other industrial countries) emerged the first working-class consumer society, a novel phenomenon which expressed itself through (for example) commercial popular music, dance halls, the music-hall and theatre, the early devel-

5 Ibid., 'History' section.

6 G. Cross and J.K. Walton, *The Playful Crowd: Pleasure Places in the Twentieth Century* (New York: Columbia University Press, 2005), Chapters 1–3.

opment of professional sport, the development of popular retailing and fashion goods (not least through the Co-operative movement), and the rise of 'fast food' in the form of fish and chips, pies and cheap confectionery (but also cheap fruit and vegetables on sale at market stalls and a multitude of back-street greengrocers).[7] Here, in grimy and polluted but hard-working and resilient industrial towns like Blackburn, Burnley and Bolton, the yeasty ferment of the Pleasure Beach's early customers worked away for fifty-one weeks in the year, to blow the cork out of the bottle of accumulated restraints and let joy be (almost) unconfined for the special fifty-second week of the year, the Wakes holidays.[8] Awareness of the watchful eyes of workmates, neighbours and Sunday School teachers ensured that the celebrations never got out of hand, and the workaday constraints on behaviour were relaxed and shifted by unspoken agreement rather than abandoned in the new setting. This made it easier for the Pleasure Beach to pursue and lay claim to respectability while purveying novelty and excitement, which is a key theme in its history, as we shall see. But the crucial point is that the new amusement park was the beneficiary of trends in popular spending power and the pursuit of commercial pleasures that were evident throughout industrial and metropolitan Britain in the late Victorian and Edwardian years, but particularly obvious and pressing in the Lancashire 'cotton towns'. The Pleasure Beach always recruited plenty of custom from beyond the county, and increasingly so in the inter-war years and beyond. Its Edwardian pulling power extended into West Yorkshire and the English Midlands, moving outwards after the First World War to Glasgow (especially) and the Scottish Lowlands, the North-East of England and even the Home Counties, Wales and the South-West; but Lancashire was, and remained, the core market that made everything else possible, and helped to sustain Blackpool Pleasure Beach's fortunes as its many rivals eventually faltered and (in most cases) declined.

But the other key word here, of course, is Blackpool; and it is impossible to separate the Pleasure Beach's fortunes from those of the town in which it grew up, and which was already well established as a popular resort at its foundation, just as the development of the world's first working-class consumer society in its Lancashire hinterland was already strongly in evidence by the late 1890s. Blackpool was, in most relevant senses, the world's first working-class seaside resort, although it was never entirely dominated by toilers in the industries of northern England, and it retained the loyalty of

7 J.K. Walton, *Lancashire: a Social History 1558–1939* (Manchester, 1987), Chapter 13; T. Griffiths, *The Lancashire working classes*, c. 1880–1930 (Oxford, 2001).

8 G. Cross (ed.), *Worktowners at Blackpool* (London, 1990).

visitors – and residents – from the comfortable middle classes as well as that of small traders and supervisory and white-collar workers, whose presence might be sufficient to justify the broader label 'popular' rather than 'working-class', although it was the manual workers who dominated numerically and set the prevailing standard.[9] Above all, it was Lancashire working-class customers that defined Blackpool's status and dominant identity, staying for several days or a week at a time and providing a long enough season to justify the building of the three piers and the huge pleasure palaces, and the great municipal investment in promenades, sea defences and other essential seaside services, which were already firmly in place when the Pleasure Beach opened for business and took its present name more than a century ago. Blackpool's great rival on the world stage, Coney Island, was a half-day tripper resort for greater New York, and although its working-class visitors from (increasingly) the poorer districts of the city far outnumbered Blackpool's in sheer numbers by the end of the nineteenth century, their fleeting visits and limited spending power were insufficient to support anything resembling the solid and permanent entertainment centres in brick, slate, iron and steel, and the streets of terraced red-brick holiday accommodation radiating from the railway termini, that marked out the confidence of Blackpool's investors in the long-term future of their resort.[10]

Blackpool already had around two million holiday visitors a year by the early 1890s, and three million or more a decade later, necessarily approximate figures that were corroborated by well-informed local contemporaries and were certainly far in advance of any English rival;[11] and its substantially built pleasure palaces, backed by popular shareholder investment capital, were already firmly in place and looking to the long haul by the end of the nineteenth century. Between the 1860s and the 1890s the Winter Gardens, the Tower and (next door) the Alhambra, the Grand Theatre and the three piers with their pavilions and pierrots, along with a myriad of smaller concerns, had already responded dramatically to the surging demand for novelty and spectacle among the industrial working (and lower middle) classes of (mainly) northern England. In many ways the pioneer entertainment enterprise had been the Raikes Hall pleasure gardens, opened in 1872 half a mile inland from the town centre, and possessing

9 P. Joyce, *Visions of the People: Industrial England and the Question of Class, 1840–1914* (Cambridge, 1991).

10 Cross and Walton, *Playful Crowd*, Chapter 1.

11 J.K. Walton. 'The Social Development of Blackpool 1788–1914', Ph.D. thesis, Lancaster University, 1974, p. 263, Table 5.2; House of Lords Record Office, evidence of Alderman Joseph Heap to the Commons Select Committee on the Blackpool Improvement Bill, 1899, Q. 408 ('We get from 3 millions to 3 and a half millions every year...').

many of the attributes of an amusement park, but on an older and more raffish model, with a dancing platform, prostitutes and (from 1874) a drinks licence covering the whole of the grounds, and featuring acrobats, firework displays and crowded spectacular re-creations of battles, Wild West shows or the exotic customs of 'savage tribes'. Perhaps significantly, Raikes Hall, a characteristic Victorian pleasure complex with its roots in the eighteenth century, went into terminal decline in the late 1890s, just as the Pleasure Beach, a classic example of the new combination of technology, participation and respectability that marked the new style of amusement park, began to get under way. By the beginning of the twentieth century the Raikes Hall site was disappearing under the new streets of a middle-class housing estate.[12] A local authority dominated by the entertainment, drink and building interests had backed these developments to the hilt, especially since the establishment of a borough council in 1876, and not least (from 1879) through a pioneering municipal advertising campaign which was able to deploy far more resources than any of Blackpool's rivals, and did so to overwhelming effect, especially by commandeering the best poster sites at a time when this was the most effective popular advertising medium. The Corporation also made repeated attempts to extend the season at either end, culminating in its highly successful investment in the autumn Illuminations from 1912 onwards, which was built upon spectacularly when wartime and post-war restrictions on electricity consumption were relaxed from 1925. But even by the time the Pleasure Beach came on the scene, Blackpool during the summer season, which embraced Easter, Whitsuntide and the period of northern town holidays that extended from July to September, had become a great regional centre for music-hall, theatre, concerts, comedy and dancing, which were combined under the same roof in great entertainment complexes such as the Winter Gardens and especially the Tower, which could add its own zoo, aquarium, roof gardens and circus to the enticing menu.[13]

So the Pleasure Beach both benefited from and built upon Blackpool's established Victorian reputation as a regional pleasure capital. Its early successes resulted from its ability to siphon off pleasure spending from the great established enterprises of the town centre, making use of the Corporation's investment in promenade extension and widening from the mid-1860s onwards, in tramway development (beginning with the first public electric street tramway in 1885), extension and updating, and in the early adoption of municipal electricity (with a demonstration of electric lighting along the

12 Walton, thesis, Chapter 6.

13 J.K. Walton, *Blackpool* (Edinburgh, 1998), Chapter 4.

promenade as early as 1879, a year after the first seaside experiment of this kind, at Portugal's Cascais)[14], to provide accessibility through mass transit and clean motive power for the exciting new rides. It also took advantage of the proximity of the third and last of the great Blackpool pleasure piers, the Victoria or South Pier, which opened in 1893 and helped to draw visitors to the tram terminus at the south end of the promenade. The Pleasure Beach's status as interloper and competitor for pennies and sixpences that might otherwise have been spent in the town centre, on the premises of powerful companies which paid heavy property taxes to the local government bodies on which their directors were highly influential, created difficulties in the early stages, as we shall see; and we should note that the first Blackpool example of a circular roller coaster, the Montagnes Russes or Russian Mountains of 1902, was set up in the grounds of the Winter Gardens, as indeed was the Gigantic Wheel of 1896. There had been various earlier roller coasters, the first primitive version being set up at Raikes Hall in 1886. As a local newspaper emphasised when introducing the Montagnes Russes as a 'Great Novelty at the Winter Gardens':[15]

> If there is anything in the world worth seeing and having you can rest assured that Blackpool will be amongst the first, if not the first, to have it. Paris, the centre of gaiety, had its Tower: Blackpool must have one too. Chicago built a Great Wheel, Blackpool followed suit. And now we are to have another world's novelty, one of the latest of Parisian playthings.

The title of one of the Mitchell and Kenyon fairground films promises an early moving picture of this Montagne Russe (so styled, in the singular); but the brief footage consists entirely of erotic cuddling scenes involving two couples on a motionless piece of machinery, a common idiom in early film, here conjuring up the seaside suspension of inhibitions in a way more suggestive of the innuendo of the comic postcard than the giddy undulations of the fairground ride itself, while reminding us in the process that the fairground ride did not have to be at the seaside to do this.[16]

The Pleasure Beach was soon to take up the running in the field of striking mechanical and technological novelties; but without the favourable environment of Blackpool, coupled with the proximity of industrial Lancashire, to incubate it during its formative years, it is hard to imagine it

[14] M. Tavares Dias and G. Alves, *Cascais 1888/1928: Aqui Nasceu o Futebol em Portugal* (Cascais: Quimera, 2004), p. 5.

[15] *Blackpool Gazette*, 13 May 1902. Thanks to Dr Vanessa Toulmin for this reference, and to Ted Lightbown for advice on early roller coasters in Blackpool.

[16] National Fairground Archive, University of Sheffield (NFA), Mitchell and Kenyon Collection, 351: *Les Montagnes Russes – Blackpool's Latest Attraction* (1902).

achieving the lasting and spectacular success that came its way. The enterprise, foresight and adaptability of the Pleasure Beach's owners, W.G. Bean and later his descendants in the Thompson family, with their capacity for hiring and nurturing the right people, were necessary to this story; but their task would have been much more difficult without this supportive and exciting environment. Other amusement parks in other resorts forged their own legends and mobilised their own devotees, but there was nothing elsewhere in Britain to match the longevity, adaptability, resilience and sheer financial success of the Blackpool enterprise.

We should also emphasise, in return, the growing importance of the Pleasure Beach to Blackpool. This is obvious from the sheer scale of the visitor numbers, and from the local authority's relationship with the amusement park, sometimes uneasy and even adversarial but, from the earliest years, recognising the economic benefits it brought to the town's economy and the Corporation's coffers. Once it had become obvious that the Pleasure Beach was an addition to the town's menu of attractions, bringing in extra visitors rather than taking them away from town centre attractions like the Tower and Winter Gardens, it became an accepted part of Blackpool's leisure economy: a competitor for tourist spending within its boundaries, but an asset in the more important external competition with rival destinations, helping to generate positive answers to the question 'Why Blackpool?' A visitor survey of the mid-1990s put this in perspective. The Pleasure Beach was 'the most important attraction or thing to do' in Blackpool for just under a quarter of respondents, rising to nearly one-third in the 16–24 age group, and well over one-third among visitors with children. More than one quarter of skilled and white-collar workers expressed this view, but just under a quarter of professional and managerial groups said the same. We shall see that some of these patterns resulted from important changes in the post-war period and the late twentieth century, with children and young people becoming more important and the better-off visitors raising their profile; and for many of those who chose to put pubs, clubs, discos and live entertainment ahead of it the Pleasure Beach would still have been an important contributor to Blackpool's attractiveness. The relationship between the Pleasure Beach and Blackpool was always two-way, and as time passed the former became increasingly important to the competitive fortunes of the latter.[17] In 1989, indeed, a sceptical Christopher Somerville described the Pleasure Beach twice in successive pages as 'Blackpool's chief bid for future survival.'[18]

[17] Hughes and Benn, 'Entertainment in Tourism: a Study of Visitors to Blackpool', Managing Leisure 2 (1997), pp. 117–8.

[18] C. Somerville, *Britain Beside the Sea* (London, 1990), pp. 215–16.

The Pleasure Beach benefits from the affection of a legion of articulate and enthusiastic fans, which shows itself in celebrations of its excitements and delights in a variety of media; and this also goes back a long way. Their appreciations can be found in hardback books and the 'serious' press, as well as in more populist outlets, and they are capable of mixing nostalgia with a lively appreciation of novelty and of the present. Here, for example, is the novelist Andrew Martin, writing about the remembered Pleasure Beach of the early 1970s in *The Observer* in June 2004:[19]

> ...the Pleasure Beach... was, and is, Europe's premier funfair, and I regret to say that no excitement of my life has ever topped approaching it on a southbound tram. It is presided over by the King of Mirth, a clownish automaton in a glass case who's been laughing hysterically since 1935. My sister and I would watch him for a while, trying to decide whether he was funny or frightening. Then it was off to the rides, especially the cavernous Fun House, a beautiful piece of modernist architecture, although that was lost on me. The relevant point was that it contained dozens of attractions for the price of one: there was the treacherous Shaking Floor, the treacherous Rocking Floor, the equally treacherous Drop Floor and the potentially erotic Social Mixer – a treacherous rotating floor that would pitch you into the laps of strangers.

But this nostalgia for the Pleasure Beach's role in the family holidays of his youth, an aspect of the amusement park's clientele that Martin now sees (in contrast with the Pleasure Beach's website) as having given way to 'young, hedonistic day trippers', is capable of coexisting both with a celebration of the current condition of the Pleasure Beach, and with an acknowledgement of its awareness and incipient exploitation of its own history:

> I've been back most years since those childhood holidays and I always return to the Pleasure Beach, which acquired Europe's most daunting roller coaster, the Pepsi Max Big One, in 1994. A few years back, I was commissioned to write about it. Just before the 230 ft, near-vertical first drop, the press officer said something like, 'Can you make out the Isle of Man?' It was an exciting ride; so exciting that I'll never go near it again. Instead I buy a candyfloss and walk around reading the plaques attached to the rides, for even the most ephemeral-looking Pleasure Beach whirligigs turn out to have a distinguished history, lovingly chronicled... You can read the popular history of England in the names of the newer Pleasure Beach rides: Space Invader, The Spin Doctor and – as of two months ago – Bling.

[19] *The Observer*, 27 June 2004. Martin is the author of the well-researched historical novel *The Blackpool Highflyer* (London, 2004), which is partly set in late Victorian Blackpool.

I quote Andrew Martin at length because his article introduces so many themes in understanding the enduring and (so far) endlessly refreshed and renewed attractiveness of the Pleasure Beach, and its capacity for appealing to a variety of publics. In this enchanted space it is impossible to disentangle the relationship between the funny and the frightening, and the central attraction of many of the experiences is that they are 'treacherous': you cannot trust them and they are always likely to surprise, frighten or embarrass you, without posing a direct physical threat, or to bring you into unexpectedly close contact with a desirable, unknown other. It promises – and delivers – unbearable excitement, while, as he points out elsewhere, offering utterly conventional photographic souvenirs of the wildest rides to be shared with family and friends in the familiar comfort of home. Like the changing ways of looking at and experiencing the sea (and the mountains) as something exciting and frightening but beautiful and romantic, and ultimately safe, that made the seaside holiday possible in the eighteenth century, the Pleasure Beach domesticates fear and turns it into a desirable commodity: it offers its own version of what the late eighteenth century called the 'sublime', the shiver of fear at the idea of imagined risk or danger that carries no physical consequences.[20]

The Pleasure Beach also provides the sort of fairground food that is eaten on the hoof, with the fingers, in public, reversing the onward march of civilisation and offering the comforting indulgence of the soft, the sweet or the tasty. As well as suspending the usual certainties and constraints of the everyday world, and hinting at the 'world turned upside down' of Carnival in which all is disrupted and upturned for a short season (before, importantly, reverting to normal), the Pleasure Beach supplies its own routines, reassurances and restraints for those patrons who return regularly in the company of family, friends, workmates and neighbours.[21] It even, as Martin points out, makes regular gestures towards conventional 'high culture': some of its 'modernist' architecture is capable of appealing to highbrow artistic tastes as well as just being enjoyed on its own terms, while the romantic view of distant scenery (the Isle of Man) is part of the envisaged attractions (however implausible) of the 'Big One'. Meanwhile, the Pleasure Beach, like Blackpool as a whole, is increasingly conscious and commemorative of its own history, merging the nostalgic attractions of the industrial museum with the up-to-date thrills of state of the art amusement technology. It is also, incidentally, a very British attraction, despite the important influences

20 A. Corbin, *The Lure of the Sea* (London, 1994).

21 Darren Webb, 'Bakhtin at the Seaside: Utopia, Modernity and the Carnivalesque', *Theory Culture and Society* 22 (2005), pp. 121–38.

of American amusement technology and the constant transatlantic negotiation in the world of the amusement park across more than a century. This is not Disney, whose obsession with conformity, control and a particular version of imagined history as progress could not be transplanted to a British setting; and when the circus proprietor Billy Smart considered setting up a syndicate to provide a Blackpool version of Disneyland in 1961, the proposed attractions had a distinctively British, European and post-imperial flavour. Walt Disney himself was not interested, and projected attendances were insufficient, kept down by the local climate, so the project was abandoned.[22] The Pleasure Beach has proved impervious to such problems and, like Blackpool as a whole, is capable of being many things to many people, and of appealing to different facets of the same person at different times; and Martin, along with many other commentators through the years, astutely highlights this ability to 'square the circle'. This is, and has been, at the core of its enduring popularity, as we shall see.

Not that the Pleasure Beach is, or has been, universally popular among those who write about it. It has generated its share of disdain and even disgust. A representative recent critique is that of Charles Jennings, a Londoner who chose to represent himself as a foreigner exploring in an alien northern England, and whose attitude to Blackpool was encapsulated as follows: 'Blackpool is the first place I've been to where the whole town has halitosis... The whole settlement reeks of chip fat, beer and ice-cream, uniformly and without let-up.' He described the Pleasure Beach as 'forty-two acres of fairground rides and vomit-inducing white-knuckle experiences', and he noted the culture of commemoration surrounding the older rides with their informative plaques only to comment sourly that, 'I can't believe that the mob which gradually descended on the Pleasure Beach after opening time was wholly comprised *(sic)* of industrial archaeologists, so I suppose the antique nature of some of the rides is immaterial to most people. To be honest, there was hardly a normal person to be seen there. Almost everyone was grossly fat or appeared to have been sleeping rough...' Determined not to spend any money, though impressed in spite of himself by the Pleasure Beach's efforts to market its rides, Jennings eventually fell prey to an overwhelming sense of revulsion and left the amusement park, and Blackpool, in disgust.[23] Several visitors in the late twentieth century from outside the Blackpool tradition have expressed similar sentiments, including such well-known international authors as Paul Theroux and Bill Bryson.

22 Cross and Walton, *Playful Crowd*, Chapter 5 and pp. 206–8.
23 Charles Jennings, *Up North: Travels Beyond the Watford Gap* (London, 1995), pp. 82, 97–100.

Over the years, and at the present time, the enthusiastic responses outweigh the disgusted ones, as a survey of current review and commentary websites suggests.[24] There is, however, limited colonisation of the middle ground between the extremes: most people seem either to love the Pleasure Beach or to hate it, although the journalist Graham Turner, in his excellent profile of Blackpool in 1967, managed to avoid the subject altogether apart from a short paragraph on the managing director Leonard Thompson.[25] Here again, it is impossible to separate reactions to the amusement park from attitudes to Blackpool as a whole; and this underlines the importance of the relationship to the Pleasure Beach's long-term success.

To set this in perspective, we need to remember that Blackpool Pleasure Beach was not the first amusement park, and that it had recognisable precursors even in the resort itself. Its roots can be found in the traditions of the travelling fairground, the county show and the international exhibition, and its ancestry is Scandinavian and American, with a distant admixture of Russian, as well as British. The Russian Mountain was indeed a Russian phenomenon, a toboggan ride from the seventeenth century, adopted in a wheeled version in Paris at the beginning of the nineteenth in an unusual reversal of the assumed west-to-east direction of European cultural influence at the time. An alternative genealogy of the roller coaster identifies it with the recreational use of the inclined planes of defunct mines at Mauch Chunk in Pennsylvania in 1870, converted into a commercial ride by the American inventor LaMarcus Thompson in 1884.[26] A further version emphasizes that the Thompson innovation, which has been given most attention in the literature, was part of a flurry of patenting activity in the area of inclined railways and roller coasters during the 1870s and 1880s, with relevant patents issued in 1872 and 1878 before a cluster of contenders coincided with Thompson in 1884. This reinterpretation demonstrates that the roller coaster's time had come, and that Thompson's success was more an expression of the 'spirit of the age' than a revolutionary new development.[27] The ancestry of the amusement park more generally, as opposed to this emblematic piece of equipment, can be traced back to Bakken Park and Tivoli Gardens in Denmark, somewhat imaginatively to 1583 in the former

24 For example www.tripadvisor.com accessed 6 January 2006.

25 Graham Turner, *The North Country* (London, 1967), p. 138.

26 Karen R. Jones and John Wills, *The Invention of the Park* (Cambridge, 2005), p. 92; Cross and Walton, *Playful Crowd*, p. 33.

27 Victor Canfield, essay on the history of roller-coaster patents (2001), www.personal.psu.edu/faculty/v/a/vac3/history.html accessed 25 Aug. 2006.

case, while Vienna's Prater had its amusement area by 1766.[28] It does depend on what you mean by an amusement park, and the exciting mechanical rides, as opposed to other forms of outdoor entertainment, came in from the 1880s onwards. They were pioneered on the travelling fairgrounds that also operated at the forefront of outdoor entertainment technology in Victorian England, and had their own influence on the Pleasure Beach and its peers.[29] As this suggests, the amusement park was never necessarily or exclusively a seaside phenomenon, as British examples from London's Vauxhall (1661), Cremorne and Ranelagh Gardens between the seventeenth and the nineteenth centuries, to Manchester's Belle Vue and Sydenham's Crystal Palace in the nineteenth and twentieth, and Staffordshire's Alton Towers in the twentieth and twenty-first illustrate very clearly. In 1908 an abortive scheme to open six purpose-built 'Coney Island' amusement parks in Britain ignored the seaside altogether, the favoured cities being London, Liverpool, Glasgow, Dublin, Cardiff and Leeds, although the proposed combination of a fairground with a 'big stage show' and assorted indoor novelties suggests that year-round custom on a large scale would have been essential to financial success. In any event, the project (which may have been the same as the six 'Mammoth Fun Cities' that were being projected with American investment a year earlier) never got beyond the drawing board. Of course, many of the Pleasure Beach's liveliest competitors were in British seaside resorts, from Southend and Margate in the south-east to Weston-super-Mare and Porthcawl in the south-west, and from Blackpool's Irish Sea neighbours at New Brighton, Southport and Morecambe to Cleethorpes and Whitley Bay on the North Sea coast.[30] On the more up-market south coast, however, Brighton and Bournemouth, which with Blackpool and Southend were the largest seaside resorts in twentieth-century Britain, had no Pleasure Beach equivalent. And the international exhibitions, especially from the Chicago Columbian Exposition of 1893 onwards, set standards for leisure architec-

[28] Jones and Wills, *Invention of the Park*, pp. 92–3; A. Theve *et al.*, *Folkets Grona Lund* (Djurgarden, 2003), p. 7.

[29] NFA on-line catalogue, essays by Vanessa Toulmin on the history of pleasure fairs and fairground technology, www.shef.ac.uk/uni/projects/nfa

[30] W. Wroth, *The London Pleasure Gardens of the Eighteenth Century* (London, 1896); M. Ogborn, *Spaces of Modernity: London Geographies, 1680–1780* (New York, 1998); L. Nead, *Victorian Babylon* (New Haven, 2000); H. Pussard, '"50 Places Rolled into One": The Development of Domestic Tourism at Pleasure Grounds in Inter-War England', in J.K. Walton (ed.), *Histories of Tourism* (Clevedon, 2005), pp. 195–210; M.J. Fisher, *Alton Towers: a Gothic Wonderland* (Stafford, 1999); *The World's Fair*, 10 Aug. 1907, 10 Oct. 1908 (with thanks to Tim Neal); N. Evans, *Dreamland Remembered* (Margate, 2003); K. Crowe, *Kursaal Memories* (St Albans, 2003); S. Copnall, *Pleasureland Memories* (St Albans, 2005).

ture and planning in parkland settings, and offered sites for pioneering rides and attractions, that had nothing to do with the seaside in itself but were readily assimilated to its amusement parks. The British international exhibitions did not find room for amusement parks as such until the turn of the century, but Earl's Court, Olympia, the White City and later Wembley played their part in subsequent developments.[31]

Blackpool had its own precursors of the Pleasure Beach, on a smaller scale. Raikes Hall, with its medley of outdoor attractions on a sprawling site, is the most obvious one, not least because it gave way to a housing estate even as the Pleasure Beach emerged. It was the Winter Gardens, in many ways a more conventional 'pleasure palace', whose grounds played host to the Gigantic Wheel of 1896 (and for more than thirty years afterwards), and the Montagnes Russes six years later; and the Tower's bill of fare, in terms of spectacles and exhibitions, overlapped with that of the Pleasure Beach even though it was all indoors and an admission fee was charged for access to the premises. On a smaller scale, pleasure grounds sprang up on the urban fringe from Blackpool's earliest days as a popular resort. Uncle Tom's Cabin, a beerhouse on the cliffs just beyond what became the northern borough boundary, gained a reputation for dancing, shooting galleries and fairground entertainments from about 1860, and Blackpool's own Belle Vue Gardens, on an inland site at Whitegate Lane, kept pace with it, perhaps providing the inspiration for Raikes Hall, alongside smaller suburban 'strawberry gardens' with a lower profile or a shorter life. By 1875 this seaside Belle Vue offered fireworks and tightrope walkers alongside bowls (an important Blackpool attraction) and archery, while the Cabin had acrobats and clog- and skipping-rope dancers. Five years later both provided dancing, indoors as well as out, and the Cabin acquired swings, roundabouts, switchbacks and an aerial flight during the 1880s, approximating ever more closely to what the Pleasure Beach was soon to become. The South Shore amusement park built on firm foundations in popular taste and entrepreneurial precedent.[32]

The Pleasure Beach also exhibited a vitality and adaptability that enabled it not only to outlive similar (and competing) amusement parks in other areas of Britain and the world, but also to flourish while they declined and disappeared. The contrast with the New York resort of Coney Island, the Pleasure Beach's coeval, source of inspiration and distant rival at the turn of

[31] P. Greenhalgh, *Ephemeral Vistas* (Manchester, 1988); N. Bolotin and C. Laing, *The World's Columbian Exposition* (Washington, D.C., 1992); J. Glanfield, *Earl's Court and Olympia: from Buffalo Bill to the Brits* (Stroud, 2003).

[32] Walton, thesis, pp. 309, 314–18, 323–4, 332.

the century, is particularly marked. Coney lost its last historic amusement park with the demise of Steeplechase in 1964 and was never able to fill the gap, while other American parks languished during the last third of the twentieth century. In Australia, too, Melbourne's emblematic St Kilda resort district temporarily lost its own version of Coney's Luna Park, although Sydney's equivalent did better; but it had only opened as recently as 1935, on a former industrial site in the Harbour.[33] An earlier venture, Wonderland City at Tamarama near Bondi Beach, opened in 1906 but survived for only five years on its cramped site straddling a small cove, in the face of local opposition and the wake of a serious accident on the distinctive Airship ride.[34] In Spain, the amusement park on Barcelona's Tibidabo, the mountain to the west of the city, was a long-term survivor. It was developed by a syndicate led by a pioneer of Spain's pharmaceutical industry, and grew up in the early twentieth century after the opening of a funicular in 1901, eventually passing into municipal ownership and retaining evocative early rides like the Atalaya and Avión, which took advantage of the panoramic views across the city.[35] A little later, at the Spanish seaside, San Sebastián's Martutene amusement park of 1910 took its cue from the American influences of Luna Park in Paris in the previous year, but, like Wonderland City, failed to survive the First World War, as did a less ambitious park on the seaside summit of Monte Ulía. A later and more populist incarnation on the Martutene site, the Campos Eliseos of 1929, lasted a few years longer, and a small amusement park on Monte Igueldo, opened out in 1912 by a funicular, survived strongly into the twenty-first century. But there was nothing in this pioneer Spanish seaside resort to match the developments at Blackpool.[36] In Britain the decline and fall of Margate's Dreamland, Southend's Kursaal and what became Morecambe's Frontierland, among others, in the late twentieth century, and the failure of survivors like Southport's Pleasureland to make a major impact on the fortunes of 'their' resorts to match that of the Pleasure Beach on Blackpool, stands in stark contrast with the persisting vigour and emblematic significance of the Pleasure Beach itself. There is something here to explain (not least because

33 Cross and Walton, *Playful Crowd*, Chapter 4; J. K. Walton, 'Popular playgrounds: Blackpool and Coney Island, c. 1880–1970', *Manchester Region History Review* 17 (2004), 51–61; M. Immerso, *Coney Island: the People's Playground* (New Brunswick, 2002); P. Spearritt, *Sydney's Century* (Sydney, 2000), p. 221.

34 Joan Lawrence and Alan Sharpe (eds.), *Pictorial History: Eastern Suburbs* (Alexandria, NSW, 1999), pp. 109–11.

35 http://www.achus.net/tibidabo/historia.htm accessed 4 Nov. 2006.

36 L. Gómez Beldarrain, *San Sebastián: Historia de los Parques de Recreo a través de la Tarjeta Postal* (San Sebastián, 2005), pp. 89–127.

the Pleasure Beach itself presided over the demise first of Frontierland, then (in 2006) of Pleasureland), as well as a strong story to tell; and this mission to explain and assess significance, as well as to describe and tell stories, will dominate what follows, beginning with the origins of the Pleasure Beach in a rapidly-developing turn of the century Blackpool.

# 2 Creating the Pleasure Beach

The Pleasure Beach, as it came into being in the 1890s (although the fairground in the sand dunes did not advertise itself under that name until 1905), was something new in the history of Blackpool's entertainments. It emerged during the second half of a particularly dynamic decade for new investment in Blackpool's popular entertainment industry, as the resident population doubled and the Tower, Alhambra, Gigantic Wheel, Grand Theatre and Victoria Pier came on the crowded scene to jostle competitively for the trippers' sixpences. But it was not a distinctive or imposing building like the Tower, the Winter Gardens, the Alhambra or the Grand, on their central sites close to the railway terminals, where the day-trippers and holiday visitors arrived and where the teeming streets of red brick shops and lodging-houses already dominated the scene. These magnificent 'pleasure palaces' housed fairground novelties alongside their more formal entertainments, and in 1896, as we saw, the Winter Gardens found room for a Gigantic Wheel in its grounds; but the shows, exhibitions, circuses, dance floors and bars were the main attractions and generators of profit. The Pleasure Beach, now and for a century to come, provided no emblematic accent on the skyline on the scale of the Tower or the Wheel to proclaim to expectant arrivals that here, at last, was Blackpool, although some of its rides made an exciting impression on their local surroundings.[1] Unlike the 'pleasure palaces', too, it was not the product of a limited company, although it later spawned several, and it enduringly lacked any pretensions to being a nominal 'shareholder democracy' like the Tower, the Alhambra, the Winter Gardens and the piers, all of which had their armies of small shareholders of relatively humble origins. On the Pleasure Beach the original syndicates soon gave way to an impressively large and enterprising family business with no parallel elsewhere in the town's entertainment industry, however influential in local politics the Bickerstaffe and Nickson brothers,[2] and the other holders of interlocking directorships in drink, transport and entertainment, might be. Nor did the Pleasure Beach emulate the piers by engaging actively with the sea and providing shows and spectacle that were

1 Gary Cross (ed.), *Worktowners at Blackpool* (Routledge, 1990).

2 J.K. Walton, 'Municipal government and the holiday industry in Blackpool, 1876–1914', in J.K. Walton and J. Walvin (eds.), *Leisure in Britain 1780–1939* (Manchester University Press, 1983), pp. 158–85.

**Before the Pleasure Beach: fairground activity on James Cardwell's land at South Shore, looking south-eastwards from the sea, just before the stalls and shows on this site were suppressed. The camel on the left dates the picture: these rivals to the donkeys did not survive beyond their single season in 1897. Notice the scattered housing and the transitional nature of the site: building development was still continuing in this area.**

suspended on planks and girders above the no man's land between shore and sea, where the tides went to and fro and the usual rules of politeness and respectability might sometimes be suspended or at least relaxed. The piers themselves might go beyond dancing and musical entertainments to provide sideshows, 'what the butler saw' machines and fairground rides, like the Central Pier's Grotto Railway in the early twentieth century; but that was not their main business.

Nor was the Pleasure Beach actually, in the fullest sense, a beach, although the sand dunes on which it was sited lay beyond the town's sea defences (and close to its southern boundary) at this time, and the site was vulnerable to flooding, as the elements sometimes demonstrated. Early photographs show high tides lapping up towards the unprotected fairground, and even after the Corporation's southward extension of promenade and sea defences after the First World War it might still be inundated in a severe storm, as occurred in 1927 and again in 1977.[3] But the Pleasure Beach was not like the earlier 'fairground on the sands', concentrated between high and low tide on the beach between the Central and North Piers, which the local authority eventually managed to regulate in 1897 after a generation of conflict, pacifying local tradesmen by charging rents for the remaining pitches from 1902 onwards, because there was nothing debatable about the land on which it stood: its attractions were firmly

3 P. Bennett, *A Century of Fun*, (Blackpool: Pleasure Beach, 1996), p. 52.

**The Pleasure Beach towards high tide in 1913, with an array of amusement machinery including the Sir Hiram Maxim Captive Flying Machine, House of Nonsense and Rainbow Wheel. Notice the donkeys on a shoreline which seems dangerously close to the amusement park itself, and the orderly queues for the rides.**

grounded in the South Shore sand dunes and did not have to be dismantled every time the tide came in. Unlike the tidal beach, there was no doubt that the land was part of the local government district and could be taxed and regulated by the Town Hall accordingly. And it soon became clear that the Pleasure Beach was going to develop on a much larger scale than the steam roundabouts and fortune-telling booths that were migrating from the beach to the front gardens of the central promenade and beginning to form the 'Golden Mile'; or than the pleasure gardens on the urban fringe that were developing a range of outdoor entertainments during the 1870s and 1880s; or even than the little clusters of stalls and amusement machinery that regularly colonised vacant lots in other parts of town during the 1880s and 1890s until developers or Corporation officials moved them on.[4] These transient miniature fairgrounds tended to be close to the town centre, on valuable building land in areas that the authorities were anxious to control; and when at the beginning of the twentieth century an 'Anglo-American syndicate', whose relationship with the Pleasure Beach promoters is not clear, tried to set up a more permanent fairground near the Corporation's own Gynn Estate, at the up-market northern end of Blackpool, it was strangled at birth by the local authority's rejection of its

4 Walton, thesis, pp. 397–9, 403–9.

building plans.[5] A similar development further north along the cliffs, in the adjoining local government district of Bispham, was able to flourish for a few years before the local authority bought the land and closed it down.[6]

Popular demand for fairground entertainment and novelty rides was already strong and visible in Blackpool in the late nineteenth century; but the Pleasure Beach appeared where it did because of a combination of cheap land (owing to vulnerability to tidal flooding through lack of sea defences), accessibility (because it was close to the terminal of the electric tramway which had run along the promenade since 1885), and the development of new kinds of amusement technology, together with the willingness of the authorities to tolerate this kind of development here but not elsewhere. The development of a disreputable district of shows and stalls, including freaks, monsters and thinly disguised fortune telling by 'phrenologists' and assorted occult practitioners, not to mention contraceptive advice, was grudgingly accepted along what was becoming the 'Golden Mile', but here land was so expensive and buildings already so tightly packed that there was no room for the development of the more relaxed, loosely-knit complex of smaller and more scattered attractions that was the hallmark of the new style of amusement park.[7] South Shore was developing its suburban residential areas, but since the 1860s and the advent of the Claremont Park estate, with its crescent facing the sea and its flagship Imperial Hotel on the northern cliffs, the 'best end' of Blackpool had been the North Shore; and by investing in sea defences, cliff walks and finally a strategically sited building estate at that end of town during the 1890s, the local authority had committed itself (and the personal fortunes of some of its leading local politicians) to this vision of Blackpool's future. South Shore was a more complex place, and it lacked large estates with influential owners who were committed to up-market development on a wider stage. Under these conditions the fairgrounds that were to mutate into the Pleasure Beach were able to consolidate their footing.[8]

Apart from the gypsies who had set up camp in the sand dunes for half a century, and whose tents had become a place of pilgrimage for seekers after the exotic (including the telling of fortunes), the sand dunes beyond the South or Victoria Pier, which opened in 1893, and the adjacent tram terminal were mainly a haven for courting couples until (and after) the fairground rides began to proliferate, at first in small-scale and very informal

5 *Blackpool Gazette* 15 May 1903; Lancashire County Record Office (LCRO), Preston, CBBl Building Plans Committee, 9 Sept. 1903.

6 LCRO, UDBa/1/1, 22 Aug. 1905.

7 Owen Davies, *Witchcraft, Magic and Culture, 1736–1951* (Manchester, 1999), pp. 253–7.

8 Walton, thesis, Chapter 1.

ventures.[9] The first recognition of the area's potential for substantial amusement park development came in the late 1880s, and precipitated a conflict between residential and commercial entertainment interests whose initial outcome, briefly, favoured the former. The key figure was James Cardwell, a self-made local brickmaker, builder and developer. He was a Conservative politician on the Council and three times Mayor in the 1890s, and was heavily involved in the land deals of that busy decade, when the town's census population more than doubled. Cardwell played his part in the shady dealings of the Gynn Syndicate, a classic Blackpool arrangement whereby well-connected businessmen bought strategically sited land that the Corporation needed for sea defence work on the northern cliffs, selling it on at an inflated profit, under circumstances that hinted strongly at collusion and conflict of interest.[10] At the other end of town, from 1882 onwards Cardwell had developed his Windsor Estate on land almost opposite what was to become the site of the new Victoria Pier, at the southern end of the existing promenade, just above the sand dunes on which the Pleasure Beach was soon to take root.[11] The horse bus and tram terminals here were thronged in the season by joy-riding trippers wanting something to do before returning to the town centre, and from about 1887 onwards Cardwell provided it, leasing the land between the sea and the respectable streets of his new estate to stallholders and showmen. It is not clear why Cardwell did not develop this prime site with dwelling houses or shops, but the mid to late 1880s were transitional years in Blackpool's development, as its growth was retarded by uncertainty about the future balance between middle-class and working-class visitors, while trading conditions in the Lancashire cotton towns were temporarily depressed.[12]

As it turned out, Cardwell's temporary arrangements worked greatly to his advantage: the Windsor Estate residents campaigned vigorously for the Corporation to step in and suppress the fairground, alleging that respectable residents and visitors were being driven away from the area, and in 1896 the Corporation paid Cardwell £10,000 for the contentious plot of land, which represented a handsome profit after he had originally paid £1850 for the whole estate. The Corporation's pretext for this transaction was that the land was needed for promenade extension, and although the original plan was that the existing streets should be extended across it and built up to a high specification, the plot was actually made into the small

9 Cross and Walton, *Playful Crowd*, pp. 68, 273–4.
10 Walton, 'Municipal government', pp. 169–70.
11 LCRO CBBl/2/17.
12 Walton, thesis, p. 87.

ornamental garden that still occupies the site.[13] Cardwell's protestations that he only made £40 per year in rent from the stalls and shows, and had philanthropically resisted an offer £3000 higher from a water-chute and fairground company, in order to appease the neighbours and protect the 'social tone' of the area, were received with scepticism and hints that these claims smacked of blackmail on his part; and shortly afterwards his local political career went into eclipse as the Gynn Syndicate scandal also erupted. But Cardwell's ability to make short-term profits out of his fairground rentals, together with the apparent plausibility of his claim about the perceived value of the land as a permanent fairground site, demonstrates the changes and opportunities that were emerging in this area.[14] They were further underlined by speculation in the local press in September 1895 about proposals by a 'London syndicate' to set up a 300-foot 'Ferris Wheel', modelled on the famous exhibit at the recent Chicago World's Fair, near the Star Inn at the far end of what was to become the Pleasure Beach site; and although a version of this proposal became the Gigantic Wheel at the Winter Gardens in the next year, the suggestion reinforced the impression that great things were possible among the southern sand dunes.[15]

The fairground was banished from the Windsor Estate in 1897, but only after a petition of 200 ratepayers against its continuation under Corporation ownership. At the same time the stalls and shows on the central beach were brought under local authority control, purged of 'offensive' elements (including phrenologists, palmists, 'chiropodists' or corn cutters, photographers, primitive cinema operators and auctioneers, but also people selling fruit, toys, jewellery, fancy goods and confectionery in competition with local shopkeepers), and greatly reduced in number from the 316 who had 'standings on the foreshore' in 1895.[16] At this point the South Shore entertainments were mainly the traditional offerings of the Lancashire town summer fair: peepshows, exhibitions (fat bullocks, giantesses...), shooting galleries, phrenologists and hot pea saloons; and the first response of their owners was to move on to the beach near the new Victoria Pier, where they were joined by some of the refugees from the central beach clearances, although most of these migrated on to the shore around Central Pier, rein-

13 Blackpool Corporation deeds, Bundle 20/27, consulted at Blackpool Town Hall.

14 Walton, 'Municipal government'; National Archives, MH12/5806, R. Walton to Local Government Board, 18 July 1896; LCRO CBBl, Highway Committee minutes, Sept. 1895 – Dec. 1897; *Blackpool Times*, 15 July 1896; *Blackpool Gazette*, 16 Aug, 1895, 13 Sept. 1895, 19 Feb. 1897.

15 *Blackpool Gazette*, 14 June 1895.

16 LCRO CBBl, Watch Committee minutes, 21 May 1897; National Archives, MH12/5804, 27 Dec. 1895.

forcing the early 'Golden Mile'.[17] This was a temporary measure, not least because the Corporation now had the power to regulate and collect rents on this area of shoreline as well as the central beach; and the showmen's more permanent response was to relocate to dry land a short distance to the south, to Watson's Estate, on what was to become the site of the Pleasure Beach. As might be expected, developments here were also controversial, and for the first decade of fairground activity in this area the operators' position was precarious.

The origins of the Pleasure Beach on part of its present site can thus be dated to the last years of the nineteenth century, although its roots in other parts of Blackpool lie deeper. The original partnership that sub-leased 20 acres of Watson's Estate for a fairground in 1897 was an interesting combination of people: Albert Ellis, a phrenologist, fortune-teller and general occultist with a well-established family business on what was becoming the 'Golden Mile' at South Beach, represented the less reputable side of the small-scale local entertainment industry, while J.W. Outhwaite was a Yorkshireman from Shipley, near Bradford, who had his own transatlantic connections: he was rescued from his business difficulties as a Blackpool butcher by his father-in-law, who had a fairground ride business in Philadelphia and supplied the carousel or roundabout that Outhwaite began to operate on the southern sand-hills in 1895, and on which his fortune was to be founded.[18] The partnership was established only two years after Paul Boyton opened Sea Lion Park at Coney Island, which is usually seen as the world's first permanent amusement park (although this does depend on the preferred definition: Copenhagen's Tivoli Gardens goes back to 1843, for example); and it coincided with the opening of George Tilyou's famous Steeplechase at the New York resort.[19] The Ellis and Outhwaite partnership soon spawned its own network of tenants and subtenants, operating a variety of rides and concessions, and became the basis of the Pleasure Beach. The gypsies who had been the first occupants of the site soon adapted to the new opportunities, and Sylvester Boswell remembered the first roundabout and bicycle railway at the turn of the century:[20]

> Now another amusement on the beach at that time, as I remember, was one old set of Gallopers... And there used to be a figure-board and if you

[17] Walton, thesis, pp. 405–9; R. Poole, *The Lancashire Wakes Holidays* (Preston, 1994).

[18] Bennett, *Century of Fun*, pp. 16–17.

[19] Cross and Walton, *Playful Crowd*, pp. 39, 45.

[20] S.G. Boswell, *The Book of Boswell* (London, 1970), quoted by Dorothy Brotherton, 'The Pleasure Beach', in Bob Dobson and Dorothy Brotherton (eds), *Fresh Air and Fun* (Blackpool, 1988), p. 96.

> rode on the outside – on the third row of horses – and you reached out, there was some rings on this figure-board, and if you could put your finger in a ring and show it to the man who took the money, you could get an extra ride. And there was another sort of Galloper-track – but with bicycles on it three abreast- and people used to get on this and pedal themselves along, and the more people that was on, the faster they went. And that was a penny a ride.

For the Pleasure Beach to develop further from these primitive origins, it needed a stronger injection of outside investment; and the real impetus to growth from something resembling a traditional fairground by the sea to a permanent amusement park using complex, expensive and solidly-founded electrical machinery, was provided by Outhwaite's father-in-law, who headed up an Anglo-American syndicate which leased just under 40 acres of Watson's Estate in 1901, with 500 yards of sea frontage, and completed its purchase in December 1904. What relationship this bore to the rumours in December 1903 of a projected 'World's Fair' on about 22 acres of Watson's Estate, to be purchased for around £30,000, remains uncertain, as does the question of whether the Walsall-based touring fairground showman Pat Collins was an unsuccessful competitor for the exploitation of the estate. But it is clear that the southern sand dunes had become a hot property by the beginning of the new century. Conveniently, the estate had come up for sub-division and sale after two of the five joint owners had petitioned for this outcome in 1898 in order to realise their assets, and without the availability of the land at this time events might have taken a very different course. The syndicate's front man and manager, William George Bean, who was actively involved in the purchase arrangements from an early stage, proved to be the true founder of the Pleasure Beach and the mastermind of its spectacular development over the next generation.[21]

Bean was a Londoner, born in Chelsea in 1868; but he had moved to the United States at the age of 19, worked in advertising in New York, and found his way into the Philadelphia amusement machinery industry in which Outhwaite's father-in-law was also involved. He returned to England in the mid-1890s with the British rights to the primitive Hotchkiss bicycle railway, an invention of 1892 which had been a commercial failure at the Chicago Columbian Exposition of 1893 and seems to

21 Walton, thesis, p. 327; Blackpool Corporation deeds, Bundle 50/22/1; *Blackpool Gazette*, 4 Dec. 1903, 14 Mar. 1911; Pleasure Beach Archives, Cuttings Books, 1928–9, pp. 98–100, June 1929; Bennett, *Century of Fun*, pp. 17–18, which tells a slightly different detailed story without benefit of footnote.

have done little better at other venues in the United States. In 1896 he used the expertise and contacts of his London stockbroker brother to set up a bicycle railway company in Britain, and operated the Hotchkiss system on tracks at Brighton and Great Yarmouth before setting up a Blackpool operation under a manager in the same year. By 1902, when he married a Great Yarmouth woman, Bean was firmly established in Blackpool, and it was not surprising that he should join forces with Outhwaite, as they operated their own rides on the Watson's Estate land and rented sites to others for stalls and mechanical rides.[22] Bean soon became the public face of the emergent Pleasure Beach, negotiating with the local authority over building plans and public order, and getting himself elected to the local council for South Shore's Waterloo Ward by a convincing majority, and with the official endorsement of the dominant Conservative group, at his second attempt in 1907. This was an impressive demonstration of the growing acceptability of what had, by this time, become known as the Pleasure Beach, after fierce attacks from local residents had threatened its future during the previous year.[23]

A further dimension of the transatlantic exchanges that lay at the heart of the Pleasure Beach's development, illustrating in the process the ways in which the rise of the British amusement park industry might blend the regional with the international, can be found in the career of John Henry Iles. This brass band promoter, editor and publicist discovered North American theme parks when he took Lancashire's Besses o' th' Barn Band on a world tour in 1906, and brought back the 'Scenic Railway', which he introduced to Blackpool and to London's White City. His subsequent career in this field took him away from Blackpool, as he became involved in amusement parks across three continents, from Berlin to Pittsburgh and from Copenhagen to Cairo, while also developing Dreamland at Margate and becoming a director of Manchester's Belle Vue, which had many of the characteristics of the Pleasure Beach (but also, for example, of the Tower) in an inland setting. But he retained ownership of the Scenic Railway, which remained a profitable concern in itself before being removed for road realignment in 1933, until his bankruptcy in 1919 enforced its sale to one of Bean's Pleasure Beach companies.[24] The possibilities for two-way

22 Bennett, *Century of Fun*, pp. 13–18.

23 Ibid., pp. 12–16; Walton, thesis, p. 512.

24 D. Russell, 'Iles, (John) Henry', in *The Oxford Dictionary of National Biography* (Oxford, 2004–5); R. Nicholls, *The Belle Vue Story* (Altrincham, 1992); H. Pussard, '"50 Places Rolled into 1": the Development of Domestic Tourism at Pleasure Grounds in Inter-War Britain', in J.K. Walton (ed.), *Histories of Tourism* (Clevedon, 2005), pp. 195–210; Bennett, *Century of Fun*, pp. 24–5.

transatlantic traffic at a humbler level are illustrated by a story told by Sir Thomas Lipton, the grocery store magnate and international yachtsman, who visited Coney Island when his yacht was anchored nearby and found that the 'Devil' in a sideshow representing Hell was taking an alarmingly friendly interest in him. It turned out that in a former phase of life 'Beelzebub' had worked in Sir Thomas's shop in Greenock, near Glasgow.[25] At all social levels, we underplay the significance of such transatlantic migrations and interchanges at our peril.

The decade between 1897 and 1907, during which Bean became the key player in the Pleasure Beach's development, was crucial to the emergence, identity and consolidation of the amusement park. It was also a period of sustained and sometimes bitter debate over the 'social tone' of Blackpool in general and South Shore in particular, as efforts were made to safeguard the 'better-class' season by prohibiting stalls and vulgar outdoor entertainments, especially in the area of the central 'Golden Mile', only to be resisted by those who made a living from the growing numbers of working-class visitors and identified the town's future prosperity with them. There was fierce rivalry between the north and south ends of the town, as local authority investment went into the North Shore while the south appeared to be neglected, and South Shore opposition to the northern schemes was vocal and outspoken at times, with occasional talk of secession.[26] Above all, there were tensions within South Shore itself, over whether to embrace or resist the growing numbers of working-class visitors. This was a theme throughout the decade of the Pleasure Beach's emergence, and the unease at the transition between holiday economies extended beyond blaming the amusement park to include all aspects of the entertainment and accommodation industries. Even the Victoria Pier, intended at the outset for a self-consciously select and discriminating clientele, found itself in two minds, when a temporary venture into variety shows at the end of the century was repudiated by the manager in 1900 as a descent into 'vulgarity' which would now be reversed by the renewed pursuit of 'respectability'. This uncertainty persisted into the new century, when the Mitchell and Kenyon film of the crowds on the pier at Whitsuntide 1904 shows knots of well-dressed and comfortably-off visitors cheek by jowl with trippers in more informal or extravagant garb. Some of the fashionable promenaders are spliced in from contemporary film of the more up-market North Pier, but there are plenty of contrasts within the South Pier footage itself. The evidence of social mixing and lack of conflict supports Blackpool's 'official'

[25] Sir Thomas J. Lipton, *Leaves from the Lipton Logs* (London, n.d.), pp. 206–7.
[26] *Blackpool Gazette*, 2 Nov. 1894, 7 Dec. 1894, 2 Oct. 1898.

view of itself as a social melting-pot in which the classes mixed in an easy and relaxed way; but alongside this cosy and comfortable image we must also consider the evidence the local press provides of transition, conflict and unease.[27]

The Pleasure Beach made its own distinctive contribution to these conflicts. It was often blamed for lowering South Shore's 'social tone', although even as the visiting public shifted down-market the respectable residential estates of suburban houses continued to spread behind the sea front. Opposition to the Pleasure Beach's early development came most stridently from the streets that were closest to the fairground. When plans were presented to the local authority to provide legal backing for a bicycle railway, steam roundabout and switchback in 1901, probably the ones that already existed on the site, it was John Hall of Burlington Road, uncomfortably close to the new developments, who led an unavailing campaign against their acceptance. The residential interest was quick to complain that the swift action against a similar fairground development at North Shore was not paralleled at the other end of town. The crisis came in 1906, when David Dickinson, significantly an estate agent, and a leading member of the South Shore Tradesmen's Association, led a campaign not only to prevent the acceptance of further building plans, but to suppress the Pleasure Beach outright. Dickinson had support from a vocal group of tradesmen who lamented the decline in the free-spending long-stay middle-class family trade which had sustained the shopping streets in the centre of the settlement, and from central business interests associated with the Tower Company who feared the new competition; but there were other voices to praise the Pleasure Beach's move to respectability and its positive contribution to a changing South Shore tourist economy. Its influence on employment and on municipal tramway and electricity profits was also becoming apparent, and by February 1907 the crisis passed, as the Corporation moved to regulate the fairground rather than suppress it. The management agreed to give up Sunday opening, to evict gypsies and other fortune-tellers, to ban mock auctions and games for money prizes, and to impose fire precautions and basic sanitary regulation, which included a main sewer twelve inches in diameter. The gypsies were important: they had helped to give the area its distinctive, edgy 'otherness' since the 1860s, and their imagined way of life, with its distinctive culture and freedom from the restraints and obligations

27 *Blackpool Gazette*, 22 June 1900; National Fairground Archive, Sheffield (NFA), Mitchell and Kenyon Collection, Reels 200, 201; J.K. Walton, 'The Seaside and the Holiday Crowd', in V. Toulmin, S. Popple and P. Russell (eds.), *The Lost World of Mitchell and Kenyon* (London, 2004), pp. 162–5; and information from Ted Lightbown.

of the settled householder, was repudiated and romanticised in almost equal measure.[28] In 1906 there were twenty permanent gypsy households on Pleasure Beach land, augmented during the summer by large numbers of itinerants. The latter were successfully discouraged, but Bean was in no hurry to get rid of his regular tenants, some of whom held Pleasure Beach concessions or worked on others. It was not until the end of 1909, after continuing pressure from the Chief Constable, that most of them were persuaded to depart, an illustration of the 'play' that was available within the system even after the agreement to regulate the fairground had been made.[29] This drives home the point that by this time the Corporation were well aware of the economic impact of the Pleasure Beach, with its £40,000 invested in permanent attractions, its electricity consumption calculated at £1300 per year, its vital contribution to the profits of the town's tramway system as it carried up to 50,000 people to the amusement park on busy summer days, and the employment it provided for 300 men every spring, preparing for the season at a quiet time in the local economy. It was rapidly becoming indispensable to Blackpool's fortunes, as the initial failure to enforce the banishment of the gypsies may have indicated.[30]

By the spring of 1907 W.H. Hampson, a senior (and unusually broad-minded) South Shore politician, was prepared to accept that the district had lost its 'better class resident visitors' for good, and also to challenge the conventional wisdom that this was due to the Pleasure Beach, pointing to the problems posed by a narrow promenade and the 'sand nuisance' as well as a nationwide decline in this market. The new working-class visitors who paid eighteen pence per night (still fifty per cent more than the minimum available in the central back streets) for basic accommodation on Station Road were the future of the holiday industry, and the problems of the shopping centre, which had lost its old customers while being by-passed by the Pleasure Beach's patrons, were counterbalanced by the growth of the residential estates.[31] But the conventional wisdom remained deep-rooted, and the establishment of a new kind of amusement park under these conditions continued to be a delicate and controversial business, not least because such a venture was associated in many minds with the unsightly stalls, ramshackle buildings and old-fashioned fairground fun of the 'carnival of the sands', which were seen as compromising the residential tranquillity and suburban

[28] D. Mayall, *Gypsy-travellers in Nineteenth-Century Society* (Cambridge, 1988); Bennett, *Century of Fun*, p. 51.

[29] Bennett, *Century of Fun*, pp. 28–9.

[30] Walton, thesis, pp. 88–90.

[31] *Blackpool Gazette*, 12 April 1907; and for Hampson see Walton, thesis, p. 529.

dignity of South Shore. Opposition did not die away overnight, although its loss of majority support was symbolised by Bean's convincing victory, at the second attempt, in the local elections of 1907. Perhaps significantly, this was the point at which the disreputable Albert Ellis, with his connections with the 'Golden Mile', fortune telling, birth control and the occult, finally severed his remaining connection with the Pleasure Beach itself, although for a few more years he continued to operate his own modest Exhibition Ground on a more southerly site near the Star Inn, where he had moved his own roller coaster to a position that blocked the anti-amusement park campaigner John Hall's sea view in 1902. Ellis was already an elected local councillor in the central Brunswick Ward, where he sat from 1902 to 1911 under the populist banner of the Municipal Reform Union, dedicated to the pursuit of economy and the eradication of corruption as well as waste, the deregulation of the popular holiday industry, and the embarrassment of local bigwigs. Bean was to prove an outspoken and sometimes controversial local councillor, but he was always far more acceptable than Ellis at a personal level, and his businesses increasingly tended towards a kind of respectability to which Ellis never aspired. The Starr Estate Company also leased out land in this area to entertainment operators, who in turn sub-let to stallholders, during these years. But the Pleasure Beach soon carved out its own distinctive identity and pulled ahead of the local competition.[32]

During the decade after 1897 the Pleasure Beach itself had been taking shape, growing, consolidating and prospering. It did not bother to advertise in the weekly *Blackpool Amusements: Official Programme of the Different Resorts* at the turn of the century, which featured various small music-halls, shops and outlying pubs, together with the Ellis Family of palmists and phrenologists, of which Albert was the head, and even a bookmaking firm based in the Netherlands, alongside such major entertainment concerns as the Tower, Winter Gardens, Raikes Hall and the Grand Theatre; but it gradually became firmly established.[33] The passing of the official plans for a bicycle railway, steam roundabout and switchback in 1901 gave it a legitimacy that set it apart from its neighbours, and in 1904 it leased a site for the Sir Hiram Maxim Captive Flying Machine, which was the first in a long line of stand-out thrill rides that gave the Pleasure Beach a strong and exciting identity and reputation. The Flying Machine was a by-product of Maxim's efforts to devise what would have been the first aeroplane, steam-powered and propeller-driven. The eccentric inventor and (continuing an important theme)

32 Walton, thesis, pp. 328, 512, 523; *Blackpool Gazette*, 3 May 1907; and information from Ted Lightbown.

33 *Blackpool Amusements*, 1897 and 1900.

assertive transatlantic businessman had put a machine weighing over three and a half tons into the air for at least 200 yards from a special track at Baldwyns Park, in Kent, in 1894, but ran out of financial backing when he needed to find another site and build a longer track for the next stage of developing controlled flight. In 1902 he returned to the idea, and decided to raise capital by marketing a fairground ride 'that would give passengers the sense of flying and climbing and descending at the will of whoever was pilot and handling the controls'. The Flying Machine had ten steel arms with a car containing several people at the end of each, to rotate from a central driving shaft at speeds of up to 65 miles per hour, rising and falling as the 'pilot' adjusted the angle of the wings. Maxim tried the machine out at the Earl's Court Exhibition of 1904, although the London County Council safety inspector insisted on the removal of the wings, which did away with the element of control (but also with potentially dangerous gravitational forces experienced by the riders) and turned the ride into 'a glorified merry-go-round'. Even in this form, it was a popular hit and financial success, and Maxim's company went ahead with further schemes for the Crystal Palace, and ('under a financial and share agreement with a Lancashire company') at Southport and Blackpool. Hence the arrival of the Flying Machine at the Pleasure Beach, where problems with its installation in the sand dunes helped to increase initial costs from £3,000 to £7,000, and a series of legal problems and disagreements with the Lancashire company led to Maxim's withdrawal from the venture. The machine on the Pleasure Beach continued to operate successfully, however, and is still in place and at work, complete with commemorative plaque and 'the original enormous driving cogs in the base', more than a century later.[34]

The Flying Machine was soon followed by further innovations, which are documented in the records of Blackpool Corporation's Building Plans Committee, as the local authority began to oversee the amusement park's development. In 1905 the helter-skelter tower, designed to look like a lighthouse and stand out alluringly on the skyline, made its first appearance, brought in from the United States. So did the extensive and exotic River Caves, another American import which also came to Blackpool via Earl's Court, after a great success at Coney Island in the previous year, and offered an 'educational' simulation of journeys through a selection of brightly-coloured caves from around the world. Approval was also given to a long list of games, sideshows and refreshment stalls. This was followed two years later, and rather belatedly, by yet another American import, the Scenic

[34] A. Hawkey, *The Amazing Hiram Maxim: an Intimate Biography* (Staplehurst: Spellmount, 2001), pp. 66–74, 103–6; Bennett, *Century of Fun*, pp. 19–21.

Railway, the Pleasure Beach's first wooden roller-coaster, which reached a height of forty feet and travelled at up to 35 miles per hour while also offering the illusion of travelling through time and space while gazing upon scenes from literature and legend. The same year saw the arrival, again from Earl's Court, of a water chute that rose to 65 feet in height and soon became immortalised through the new comic postcards. The origins of this idea,

**Looking across the beach to the Pleasure Beach of 1906, with only the Sir Hiram Maxim Captive Flying Machine and the Helter Skelter standing out on the flat skyline. The beach is overwhelmingly a female space, with children building sandcastles and taking little notice of the fairground at their backs.**

**Early developments on the Pleasure Beach site, looking south towards the Star Inn and the rival enterprise that adjoined it. The Bicycle Railway is prominent, as is the switchback and a merry-go-round. The gypsy encampment and a ramshackle collection of stalls confirm an impression of makeshift randomness.**

too, lay at Coney Island, where Dreamland had been pioneering a new kind of fantasy pleasure architecture since its opening in 1904, outdoing its established rivals in the process. The Velvet Coaster of 1909, which provided a smoother ride than its precursors, was installed by a Philadelphia amusement engineer, William H. Strickler. The Joy Wheel, which provided exciting effects for numerous spectators by throwing the participants into disarray, exposing female legs and underwear, arrived in 1910 via the Brussels Festival, but was already popular as the Human Roulette Wheel at Coney Island's Steeplechase two years earlier.[35] These years also saw the introduction of the (Brooklyn) cake walk, the 'Gee Whiz', 'the dodgers', the 'Voyage in a Submarine' and the haunted cabin, many of which continued established processes of transatlantic technological exchange which were already familiar to Lancashire people from (for example) the cotton industry, and foreshadowed or exemplified by the backgrounds of Bean, Outhwaite, Maxim and Iles. In their fairground guise they were already becoming an enduring and much-vaunted theme of Pleasure Beach operations, as Bean made regular journeys across the ocean to sustain the flow of new ideas. In 1910 Bean and Outhwaite set up the Blackpool Pleasure Beach as a limited company, with a nominal capital of £70,000, and this was followed by a series of additional companies from the same stable to pursue specific activities, beginning with the 'spectatorium' for the Monitor and Merrimac battle show, which re-created a naval engagement of the American Civil War between early 'ironclad' battleships, and had been given its first airing two years earlier at Coney Island. It was adapted to present a review of the British fleet in 1914; but more prosaic British concepts like the miniature railway, imported from the Duke of Westminster's estate at Eaton Hall, and the miniature Brooklands racing track, fared much less well. The Roller Skating Rink of 1909, however, was the successful initiative of a British entrepreneur, beating off competition within Blackpool and surviving longer than previous versions of this usually ephemeral craze, which had first flared and died thirty years earlier; and in 1916 Bean brought it in-house and kept it going for another twenty years. In 1911, as the Pleasure Beach continued to gather momentum, Outhwaite died suddenly. This did not disrupt the business, as Bean was both Chairman and Managing Director of the company, and Outhwaite's heirs were content to become sleeping partners, leaving Bean to get on with running the Pleasure Beach.[36]

35 Bennett, *Century of Fun*, pp. 24–5; Cross and Walton, *Playful Crowd*, pp. 41, 47, 70.

36 J.K. Walton, 'The Transatlantic Seaside from the 1880s to the 1930s: Blackpool and Coney Island', in N. Campbell, J. Davies and G. McKay (eds.), *Issues in Americanisation and Culture* (Edinburgh, 2004), pp. 118–19; Bennett, *Century of Fun*, pp. 31–4.

**The Pleasure Beach's vulnerability to high tides and storm damage, a product of its location beyond the promenade and sea defences, is illustrated by this photograph from 1907, looking northwards to the Tower across the debris generated by that year's high tide.**

**The Bicycle Railway in action, with the switchback and the River Caves, a recent addition to the Pleasure Beach's attractions in 1906, which offered the kind of virtual tour of exotic sites from across the world that had long been familiar from fairground shows and laid useful claim to providing that enduring staple of legitimacy, 'rational recreation'. A few respectably dressed customers walk across the sand.**

**The Witching Waves were ancestors of the Dodgems, propelled by an undulating floor of hinged plates, and offering similar opportunities for men and women to make friendly contact, as in this case soon after the First World War. The soldiers appear to be Australian, and we also see two young male Pleasure Beach workers helping to keep the cars moving and, no doubt, collecting fares.**

Profits and activities continued to expand, and by 1913 the local authority had authorised 91 plans on the site. They included the Rainbow Wheel of 1912, a lasting landmark and another scenic railway concept, but one that offered a sequence of views and sensations while the customer remained almost static. The Witching Waves, ancestors of the Dodgems, followed in 1913.[37] Most of these multiplying attractions were run by private companies under the immediate supervision of the syndicate and company, whose aim from the beginning had been to found 'a White City, or Amusement Park, on American lines'. By 1914 the Pleasure Beach had a summer staff of 600, welcoming up to 100,000 visitors on an ordinary day and 200,000 on a Bank Holiday, and laying claim to a total investment of £200,000 in its various rides and other attractions.[38] In 1913 it marked off its main entrance with a signature building, the Casino, built in an 'Indo-Classical'

[37] Bennett, *Century of Fun*, pp. 34–5.

[38] Walton, thesis, pp. 328–9; and for these two paragraphs LCRO, CBBl, Building Plans Committee, 1905–14.

style which 'echoed the imperial style of many Pleasure Beach rides' at this stage, as well as many older pieces of fantastic seaside architecture from the Brighton Pavilion onwards. The building was solidly and prosaically constructed in the new material of the era, reinforced concrete, but lavish use of external arcading and a display of electric light bulbs made it 'a fantasy palace at the end of the Promenade' at night. It contained a 700-seat cinema and a restaurant, as the Pleasure Beach diversified its offerings towards incorporating a more conventional entertainment menu.[39] Fittingly, by this time the Pleasure Beach was becoming firmly established and accepted in Blackpool, and in 1910 the *Blackpool Gazette*, mouthpiece of the local Conservatives and of the dominant groups within the popular holiday industry, gave a ringing endorsement of its new respectability: 'Out of a noisy chaos of old-fashioned stalls, roundabouts, and such things as are generally known as "all the fun of the fair", Messrs. Bean and Outhwaite have evolved an orderly and most attractive exhibition ground, containing many of the latest novelties and inventions of the showman's world.'[40] This language of 'evolution', orderliness and modernity expressed exactly the image of the Pleasure Beach that Bean, in particular, was seeking to establish. Its identification with the 'civilising process', marching in step with increasingly positive perceptions of the Blackpool holiday crowd and its behaviour, also chimed in with Bean's efforts to attract and install more permanent and well-organised structures and infrastructure to transform the fairground into a 'modern amusement park'.[41] Events in 1913 confirmed that the local authority shared the view of the dominant local newspaper on the positive nature of the changes that were taking place.

In July 1913 the Pleasure Beach's permanent presence at South Shore was further recognised and confirmed, and defined with greater clarity. The Corporation's plans for the further southern extension of the Promenade by just over a mile, which would provide sea defences and improved access for the Pleasure Beach, precipitated a formal agreement between the local authority and the company which secured the latter against competition while recognising its right to continue to develop within well-defined boundaries. The heads of agreement made clear that the Pleasure Beach was to pay its full share of the costs of the improvement, two-thirds of which were to be paid by the landowners south of the existing Promenade who would benefit from it. In return it was given the right to veto any tramway

[39] Lynne F.K. Pearson, *The People's Palaces: the Story of the Seaside Pleasure Buildings of 1870–1914* (Buckingham, 1991), p. 78.

[40] Bennett, *Century of Fun*, p. 32.

[41] There were some cross-currents in this process: Cross and Walton, *Playful Crowd*, Chapter 3.

**Looking south from the recently-installed Scenic Railway in 1907, with the rival fairground south of the Star Inn clearly visible, although far enough beyond the promenade tramway to deter all but the most curious. The circular route of the Bicycle Railway can be traced, and the incomplete sign for Thompson's Railway dominates the foreground. The gypsies are still very much in evidence.**

extension along the new promenade for fifteen years, securing it against being outflanked by competing developments to the south, such as the Fair Ground at the Star Inn, where the inventor of a 'racing marbles game' had been successfully prosecuted in 1907 for operating a game of chance. The Corporation provided further defences against competition by undertaking to secure covenants from adjoining landowners not to use their land for an amusement park. This suited both sides, as it confined fairground activity to a clearly defined area, which was to be marked out by an eight-foot fence on the southern boundary and a ten-foot wall on the western side, with no more than three openings of a maximum of thirty feet each. Within this enclosure some of the land was to be kept free of temporary buildings, but a central core area was freed from restrictions on temporary or moveable buildings, although (crucially) the whole of the Pleasure Beach was subjected to statutory sanitary regulation, and the last of the gypsies were finally to be banished. This firm definition of the Pleasure Beach's external and internal boundaries was reinforced by the Corporation's commitment to try to divert Watson's Lane so as to remove the existing public highway through the amusement park. This never came to pass, and the integrity of the site was also threatened by an option to extend Bond Street, the main South Shore shopping street, through the Pleasure Beach from north to

**The Scenic Railway, an early wooden roller coaster that was imported from the United States via London's Earl's Court. The visitors are well-dressed, and in some cases flamboyantly so, but they are still crossing the sands on boardwalks. Permanent hard surfacing is still a thing of the future.**

south. This apart, the effect of the agreement would be to seal the Pleasure Beach off from the rest of South Shore and control its surroundings, safeguarding the existing business against competition while making it easier for the owners of nearby estates to develop the kind of middle-class residential estates for commuters and the retired that were already spreading profitably through this part of Blackpool.[42]

Contemporary photographs and comment confirm the *Blackpool Gazette* view that the Pleasure Beach itself was becoming increasingly respectable. An important aspect of this was Bean's avoidance of the kind of controversial and down-market entertainment that flourished on the Golden Mile and at Coney Island, especially shows depicting heaven, hell, disaster and deformity, which flourished at Coney Island but would have been dangerously divisive in the Pleasure Beach setting.[43] As the buildings and layout became more formal and permanent, in contrast with the exotic disposability (and much greater vulnerability to fire) of the Coney Island amusement parks, so the Pleasure Beach's photographic collections suggest

[42] LCRO, CBBl council minutes, Highway Committee, 28 July 1913; *Blackpool Gazette*, 29 July 1913; Walton, thesis, pp. 51–6, 69–73.

[43] Walton, 'Transatlantic Seaside', pp. 119–20.

that crowds were well-dressed, with a mixture of young adults and older couples that matched the predominant age-ranges of working-class visitors. This was a time when few wage-earning families with young children could yet afford an extended stay in even the cheapest of Blackpool's company-houses; but the late nineteenth century had seen rising consumption standards for all but the most disadvantaged of the industrial working class in the 'cotton towns', and this was reflected in the availability of 'best clothes' for special occasions like days out and annual holidays, as people literally 'dressed up' to impress. They were also habituated to self-discipline by the imposed routines of school and work, in line with subsequent claims about the 'civilisation of the crowd' during these years; and they were sensitive to the opinions of neighbours and older workmates, especially those who had some claim to authority and respect through skilled or supervisory status or a role as, for example, lay preacher or Sunday School teacher.[44] The Pleasure Beach soon became acceptable to the Bolton socialist dialect writer Allen Clarke, an early critic of the Blackpool seaside holiday and entertainment industry, who became increasingly tolerant of commercial popular culture after he moved to the resort and began to produce *Teddy Ashton's Gradely Guide* to Blackpool, which described the Pleasure Beach in 1908 as '…a wonderfull collection of entertainments, aw i' th' open air – hobby horses, switchbacks, th' river caves, th' scenic railway, th' Spanish street…'[45]

Such acceptability was heightened by the absence of conflict between the generations. The teenager as separate, alien, disruptive and a problem was still a thing of the future at Blackpool: gangs of 'scuttlers' in distinctive garb, and similar gatherings of threatening youth, might attract attention in parts of working-class Manchester, Liverpool or Birmingham, but not yet at the seaside.[46] Adolescents as an identifiable group, with their own dress codes and mannerisms, remained invisible at the Pleasure Beach, as elsewhere in holiday Blackpool, until the late 1950s. This was a secure place for relaxation and the release of inhibitions, in the company of others not only from similar environments, but also from the same towns and workplaces. The rides and other entertainments might provide opportunities for, or even promote, screams, minor intimacies and bodily exposure, as in the

44 Walton, 'The seaside and the holiday crowd', p. 160–3; *The World's Fair*, 3 Aug. 1907: J.M. Golby and A.W. Purdue, *The Civilisation of the Crowd: Popular Culture in England 1750–1900* (London, 1984).

45 *Teddy Ashton's Gradely Guide to Blackpool* (4th edn., 1908), p. 25.

46 A. Davies, 'Youth gangs, masculinity and violence in late Victorian Manchester and Salford', *Journal of Social History* 32 (1998), pp. 349–69.

social melting-pot of the Joy Wheel or the physical excitement of the roller coaster; but the relaxation of everyday inhibitions was usually governed by a shared awareness of what was and was not permissible. At Blackpool, and at the Pleasure Beach, the conventions of everyday life were relaxed, but they were not abandoned.

We shall return to these issues in a later chapter. For the time being, we should emphasise how far the Pleasure Beach had already come during that extended if sometimes stormy summer of Edwardian England, before the generation that was captured by early Pleasure Beach photography and the Mitchell and Kenyon films marched away to war or was left to lick its wounds and mourn its losses. Some amusement parks, even Coney Island's famous but short-lived Dreamland, were already falling by the wayside; others had yet to be founded. The Pleasure Beach was already big business, carving out a clear and unique identity for itself within what was already the world's first working-class seaside resort and the most popular pleasure town in Europe, and gaining the recognition from the town's government that was necessary to secure its future. There were further conflicts to come, but Blackpool's great amusement park was already an established, and economically necessary, fact of life. It was strong enough to ride out the First World War and to defy the Depression, as we shall see in the next chapter.

# 3 A Modern Amusement Park: the Pleasure Beach between the Wars

**The Pleasure Beach's first Casino, opened for the last full season before the First World War. For a generation it was as emblematic of the amusement park as the Tower was of Blackpool as a whole. This view was taken from the south in the prosperous year of 1920, the height of the post-war boom in the Lancashire cotton industry. The 'oriental' turrets are echoed by the domes of the South Pier Pavilion, which can be seen on the left. The emphasis is firmly on the Casino's role as cinema and place of respectable refreshment.**

The Pleasure Beach, like Blackpool as a whole, weathered the First World War remarkably well. Bennett tells us that, 'Throughout the war until 1918 the gross income of the park remained constant at around £13,000, rather below the peak of £15,932 in 1913. But in 1918 it shot up to £23,379 and in 1919, the first year of peace, it nearly doubled.'[1] Inflation played a part in this, but the growth in receipts outpaced it; and 1913 had been a bumper year. New rides and new investment were placed on hold, but demand remained buoyant. Blackpool had been slow to accept the implications of the new scale of conflict and its potential to imperil British civilians, especially coastal ones, and the autumn Illuminations, which had already become highly successful in extending the season during their first two years of operation, were allowed to continue through the early weeks of the

[1] Bennett, *Century of Fun*, pp. 38–9.

war, until they were terminated by a combination of security fears and a growing sense of unseemliness at the juxtaposition of commercial festivity at the seaside and deaths at the front line. But the resort's other attractions, including the Pleasure Beach, remained emphatically open for business throughout the conflict. This even applied to the piers, which might have seemed particularly vulnerable. The restrictions that affected the south and east coasts did not apply here, and nor was there any equivalent of the naval shelling of Scarborough and Whitby. The town's holiday accommodation was used extensively for the billeting of troops in training, which in turn acted as a free advertisement, and in 1917 free-spending American servicemen arrived to join the soldiers from Australia and other parts of the Empire. There was also an important military convalescent home on the Pleasure Beach's doorstep at South Shore, and military uniforms are much in evidence in wartime photographs. Alongside all this the holiday season continued, despite the problems of allocating railway rolling stock and later organising rations. The great industrial holidays were quickly recognised as too important, for morale and efficiency alike, to be suppressed.[2]

Blackpool in wartime lost visitor custom and spending power through the absence of men in the armed forces and the controversially small allowances that were paid to their families, although miners, skilled engineers and some cotton workers were needed at home, munitions workers (including many women) were often well paid, and older age-groups with savings and without dependent families had always been important. Moreover, not only did it gain soldiers in training from beyond its established catchment area, it also benefited from the wartime problems faced by competitors, especially the Yorkshire coast, whose North Sea outlook placed it much more obviously in the front line, and above all the Isle of Man, whose lifeline was cut by the fear of enemy action and the conscription of the big passenger steamers of the Steam Packet Company for war service, and whose accommodation industry suffered extreme hardship in the war years. 634,512 passengers had arrived at the Douglas ferry terminal between 1 May and 30 September 1913, all from areas that also supplied Blackpool, a flood that dwindled immediately to a tiny trickle in wartime.[3] Blackpool was an obvious alternative destination. The loss of its own excursion steamers, which provided additional attractions for its own visitors, paled into complete insignificance by comparison, and overall there is no

2 J.K. Walton, 'Leisure towns in wartime: the impact of the First World War in Blackpool and San Sebastián', *Journal of Contemporary History* 31 (1996), pp. 603–18.

3 J. Belchem (ed.), *A New History of the Isle of Man: Vol. 5, the Modern Period, 1830–1999* (Liverpool, 2000), pp. 232, 235–6, 238–40.

doubt that the town did well out of the war. The town, and the Pleasure Beach, were also ready to make a flying start when peace returned.

Blackpool is often thought of as a Victorian resort; but in many ways its most expansive and dynamic period of growth came in the inter-war years, as its local authority invested heavily in parks, gardens, promenades, sea defences and bathing pools, and it acquired new bus and coach stations, a fleet of streamlined trams and an early multi-storey car park, a big Co-operative department store, a prominent Woolworth building on the sea front, and, on the eve of the Second World War, an opulent and self-confident new Opera House for the Winter Gardens. There were failures as well as successes: the municipal airport never took wing as expected, the ambitious central re-planning of the late 1930s was aborted by the outbreak of war, and the improvement of the Victorian sewerage system failed to materialise. The resident population probably doubled during the inter-war years. The June census of 1921 (they were usually held in early April) counted nearly 100,000 people, but once the early holidaymakers had been deducted from the total a more realistic 73,000 remained. All the indications are that the population at the outbreak of the Second World War was well over 140,000, although calculations are difficult because no census was taken in 1941. Residential estates spread along and behind the promenade extensions to north and south and coalesced in broad tree-lined avenues around the new Stanley Park, as Blackpool's commuter and retirement populations continued to grow alongside the holiday industry.[4] New hotels and guest-houses were few in number, perhaps not surprisingly in a town where the 1921 census recorded more than 5000 existing ones; and they were concentrated mainly on the new South Promenade, close to the Pleasure Beach itself, where a small 'Art Deco' enclave developed in the early 1930s.[5] Registered employment in 'entertainment and sport' increased from 1808 people in 1929 to 3005 in 1939, while that in catering and hotels shot up from 4751 to 8741 over the same decade.[6] The autumn Illuminations gathered momentum as a uniquely successful device for extending the season after their restoration in 1925, becoming steadily more elaborate and attracting increasing publicity, while visitor numbers increased to an estimated seven million per year. These were prosperous and confident years for most substantial Blackpool businesses, despite the pockets of poverty in its hinter-

4 J.K. Walton and C. O'Neill, 'Numbering the holidaymakers: the problems and possibilities of the June census of 1921 for historians of resorts', *Local Historian* 23 (1993), pp. 205–16.

5 J.K. Walton, 'The Blackpool landlady revisited', *Manchester Region History Review* 8 (1994), pp. 23–31, and author's inspection of the area.

6 Lancashire and Merseyside Industrial Development Association, *The Lancashire Coast Area* (Manchester, 1951), p. 28.

land and (especially in winter) within the town itself. But in striking contrast with the late Victorian entertainment boom, much of the key investment and innovation was municipal: apart from the Opera House, and a series of new cinemas culminating in the magnificent Odeon adjoining North Station on the eve of the Second World War, the Pleasure Beach was the only great innovator in private enterprise, at least in terms of new buildings and plant. Blackpool's 'pleasure palaces' of the late nineteenth century had been uniquely successful, with the telling exception of the Alhambra in 1899, although its problems were due more to financial miscalculation than to underestimation of demand, and it ran successfully as the Palace under Tower Company ownership between 1904 and 1961.[7] But the perils of saturating the market were visible (for example) elsewhere on the Irish Sea, especially at New Brighton, Morecambe and Douglas.[8] Blackpool's inter-war popular entertainments remained highly innovative and responsive to the preferences of their audiences, but the energy went into producing shows rather than developing new venues.[9] Under these conditions the Pleasure Beach's influence on Blackpool's politics and economy continued to grow during these years. The death of William George Bean in 1929 might have interrupted or even disrupted this process, and his successors were not to repeat his active involvement in the politics of Blackpool Corporation; but the company was fortunate to find an unexpected but very able successor waiting in the wings, in the form of Bean's son-in-law Leonard Thompson.[10]

During the difficult decades of the 1970s and 1980s there were to be more casualties among the ambitious investments of the 1920s and 1930s than among the pleasure palaces, piers, hotels and boarding-houses that dominate Blackpool's Victorian legacy; but prominent among the survivors from the inter-war years are many of those elements of the Pleasure Beach that were developed, introduced and re-made in streamlined, swooping modernist form in these difficult, fluctuating but ultimately formative and transitional decades, and especially under Leonard Thompson's innovatory regime during the 1930s. It was during these years that the Pleasure Beach, after a slow start in the conflict-ridden and resources-starved years of the war's immediate aftermath, acquired an enhanced air of permanence and

7 Walton, thesis, Chapter 6 and especially pp. 324–6.

8 J.K. Walton, *The English Seaside Resort: a Social History 1750–1914* (Leicester, 1983), pp. 175–8; Belchem (ed.), *Isle of Man*, p. 224.

9 Sue Arthur is currently working on a University of Central Lancashire Ph.D. thesis on developments in popular entertainment in Blackpool during the 1930s.

10 Bennett, *Century of Fun*, pp. 53–6; and for this paragraph in general, Walton, *Blackpool*, Chapter 5.

respectability that set it apart even more decisively from its American counterparts, and brought it full recognition as an essential part of the expanded and updated Blackpool entertainment menu of the time. It was helped by promenade extension and new building in the sand dunes on its southern side, while the magnificent South Shore swimming baths of 1923, which adjoined the South Pier just across the promenade from the Pleasure Beach, drew visitors into the vicinity (nearly 600,000 in 1925)[11] and probably complemented the amusement park rather than competing with it. The Corporation's own holiday guides soon became capable of extended and even extravagant praise, as in 1928:[12]

> Whether the visitor is young or old, I beg that he will not fail to spend an hour or two on the South Shore Pleasure Beach. If he is young, it will be his very element. If he is old it will take him back to those days when he was not yet old and will, for a time at any rate, give him back his youth. There is, I vow, every bit as great a thrill in ten minutes on the Big Dipper as there ever was on a climb of the Matterhorn, and I commend, too, that other thrill of the Velvet Coaster, or a trip through the quite unexpectedly delightful River Caves... entertainment of an entirely innocent nature.

To set this enthusiasm in context, the Corporation guide was an annual promotional publication whose main focus was not on commercial entertainment; and much less had been said about the Pleasure Beach four years earlier, although it was recognised that its 'pre-eminence is threatened only by famed Coney Island in America.'[13] Even in 1937, for example, the official guide began by emphasising Blackpool's health-giving qualities and presenting an outdoor menu involving the promenades and their extensions, the open-air baths, the beauties of Stanley Park, the golf courses and of course the beach. 'The evergreen Fylde', Blackpool's undistinguished surrounding countryside, received as much attention as the three piers and the Pleasure Beach together, although the official text emphasised that at the amusement park, 'Everything has been entirely modernized... Children have not been forgotten... there is a modern hygienic crèche', while the brand new Ice Drome with its 'super ballet on ice' was also highlighted in the brief text. The dominant visual image was the sedate and family-friendly Pleasure Beach Express miniature railway, as reintroduced

11 Bennett, *Century of Fun*, p. 47.

12 *Blackpool: Britain's Playground* (Blackpool, 1928), p. 31.

13 *Blackpool Official Guide 1924: the Home of Health, Pleasure, Fun and Fancy* (Blackpool, 1924).

using smut-free diesel traction in 1933,[14] and the panoramic views of the park's attractions featured scattered and sedate groups of respectable people strolling in front of the new modernist leisure architecture of the Fun House and Auto Skooter, with the Sir Hiram Maxim ride forming a strong accent on the skyline, alongside a 'Pleasure Beach by night' image that linked the park with the Illuminations and placed the Noah's Ark at centre stage, with only a handful of visible punters. The Pleasure Beach's own full-page advertisement, complete a with 'funny face' clown icon that recalled the emblem of Coney Island's Steeplechase park, urged visitors to 'bring all the family', 'park the new baby in the crèche', and 'park the children (and grandpa) in the kiddies' amusement park'.[15]

This was absolutely in tune with the Corporation's vision for the town's development, which sought to move up-market by attracting middle-class families from an ever-widening catchment area, laying greater stress on health, sport, nature, the outdoors and even the countryside than on the seamier side of Blackpool's 'traditional' Wakes Week entertainments on and around the 'Golden Mile'. In 1935 the Corporation's proposed promenade improvement scheme involved sunken gardens, hot-houses, a 'velvet walk' for tired feet, and areas set aside for sun-bathing, while those Central Beach sideshows and stalls that could not be abolished were to be shut away and sealed off from sensitive eyes, ears and noses. A year later C.A. MacKay, the Corporation's Attractions Manager, insisted that, 'We should adopt the methods of the Pleasure Beach. Get rid of Victorian styles. This is the reign of Edward the Eighth.' A few weeks later the relationship between MacKay, his committee and the Pleasure Beach had broken down completely, but about other matters, and the shared commitment to streamlined modernisation remained.[16]

The emphasis on fresh air, health, sport, greenery and modernity extended beyond the Corporation's own promotional material: it can be found, for example, in the independent *United Kingdom Holiday Guide*, whose 1939 edition began its Blackpool entry with promenades and gardens, devoted a surprising amount of attention to the beauties of the unremarkable surrounding villages, and began the list of 'Attractions and Amusements' with tennis, golf, bowls and putting, relegating the Pleasure Beach to the end of a cursory list of commercial entertainments. The 1928

[14] Bennett, *Century of Fun*, pp. 62–3.

[15] Blackpool Corporation, *Blackpool: open the door to holiday happiness* (Blackpool, 1937), pp. 24–5, 137; *Blackpool: Britain's Playground*, pp. 30–1.

[16] Pleasure Beach Archive, Cuttings Books, 1935–6, insert from *West Lancashire Evening Gazette*, 25 June 1935; 1935–6, p. 54.

Guide had itself laid great emphasis on the beach as children's playground, with 'thousands of gay children, light of heart in the presence of fond parents, enjoying themselves with buckets and spades and playing all manner of happy games…' Most of these children would come from the better-off families whom the Corporation sought to encourage, although in some cases, as at Coney Island, the beach would be a necessarily cheap alternative to the commercial entertainment centres. Even in the late 1930s, after the worst of the really severe depression years of the beginning of the decade were over, most working-class families still had difficulty in financing a seaside holiday, even in the cheapest Blackpool accommodation, when the children were young and unable to contribute to the budget. Paid holidays in the cotton industry were still a thing of the future, although their availability was expanding rapidly elsewhere during the 1930s. The poverty cycle still made a holiday fully attainable only for unattached young adults or child-free couples, or at the point when children started to become economic assets after leaving school and starting paid employment. Evidence from Mass-Observation in 1937 suggests that most children at the Pleasure Beach looked at the rides and had them explained by parents (all were accompanied by adults) rather than actually going on them, which suggests that many of the families with young children who could afford a Blackpool holiday had to ration their spending carefully.[17] In 1934 William Holt provided a graphic description of the constraints on spending that might be imposed on a family with young children who tried to eke out their savings for a full week, running perilously short of food over the last two or three days and spending all their time on the beach while lamenting the rash expenditure of two or three shillings on stalls and peep-shows at the start of the week. Nor did such people come by car: they would make the journey much more cheaply by train or, increasingly from the 1920s, by bus. The persisting emphasis on the beach, the promenades, sport and the outdoors in Blackpool's advertising profile cannot have helped the Pleasure Beach in gaining external publicity, despite the occasional eulogy; but it seems to have swum successfully against this tide and even tried to turn the emphasis on modern but innocent outdoor entertainment to its own advantage, especially in striving to attract a middle-class visiting public on its own account. The language of 'parking' in the Pleasure Beach advertising suggests a particular appeal to those better-off social groups that could already aspire to car ownership, while the reference to 'grandpa' combines acknowledgement of the importance of the extended family with indicat-

17 University of Sussex, Mass-Observation Archive, W56/F, 'The Pleasure Beach and Tram Rides.'

ing that the Pleasure Beach itself was still predominantly a place for adult pleasures (albeit childish ones) rather than small children or the elderly.[18]

During the 1920s, indeed, the Pleasure Beach sought to cater for families by providing segregated areas for babies and children, rather than integrating them into the mainstream entertainments of the park. This helps to explain the very limited numbers of children visible on contemporary crowd photographs of the amusement park during the 1920s and 1930s.[19] In 1924 it opened its own children's playground, complete with swings, slides, a see-saw, sand pit and paddling pool, and by 1927 it had introduced scaled-down versions of some of the adult rides, including the Flying Machine and a big wheel as well as roundabouts, a train and a miniature car track, as described in the advertisement. The crèche, complete with uniformed nurses, was added in 1936. The surviving home movies of middle-class families suggest that this policy was successful, and it was in tune with the Corporation's own preferences. The official holiday guides laid great emphasis on this aspect of the amusement park's provision.[20]

These patterns of change and development took time to emerge. In the immediate aftermath of the First World War, the Pleasure Beach returned to 'business as usual', though it took a few years for the wave of innovations that had marked the pre-war years to return to full spate. Bean supplied an immediate novelty in 1919 by encouraging the Manchester-based aviation pioneer A.V. Roe, whose core business was beginning to struggle in the post-war climate, to offer flights in four biplanes, using land provided free of charge on a site adjoining the Pleasure Beach. By mid-September Roe's pilots were making 500 passenger flights a day, at prices that began at a guinea (£1.05, and a unit of currency that carried aristocratic associations) for ten minutes; and this attraction remained on the menu into the mid 1920s. Not only did this illustrate the spending power of a significant number of Blackpool's visitors, when the maximum cost of an amusement park ride was still sixpence (2.5p) and a night's accommodation in a decent guest-house was available for three shillings (15p): it also brought crowds of spectators to the Pleasure Beach, many of whom then became additional customers, at no cost to Bean himself.[21]

18 Susan Barton, *Working-class Organisations and Popular Tourism 1840–1970* (Manchester, 2005), Chapters 4–5; *United Kingdom Holiday Guide: Where to Go and What to See* (London, 1939), pp. 76–7; William Holt, 'I Watch the North on Holiday', *Daily Dispatch*, 3 Aug, 1934, p. 12.

19 Cross and Walton, *Playful Crowd*, p. 123; Pleasure Beach Archive, photographic collection.

20 Blackpool Pleasure Beach Archives, Folder 9; North West Film Archive, Manchester, No. 152, 'A Holiday in Blackpool', 1934; Bennett, *Century of Fun*, p. 46.

21 Bennett, *Century of Fun*, p. 40.

Consolidation on the basis of the existing attractions was otherwise the order of the day during the war and its immediate aftermath, aided by the beneficial consequences for Blackpool of the great post-war boom in the cotton industry, which reached a spectacular peak in 1920, when some firms were paying dividends of 40 per cent, only to fizzle out into lasting depression in the following year.[22] Blackpool's entertainment companies also paid unprecedented dividends at this time, and the Pleasure Beach's profits easily exceeded the record year of 1919 as it challenged the Tower Company for local primacy. The agreement with Blackpool Council in 1913 had been incorporated into the Blackpool Improvement Act of 1917, after complex further negotiations, and in 1921 a period of sustained disruption to the Pleasure Beach's seaward surroundings began, as work on the new promenade and swimming pool got under way.[23] Bean occupied himself by forming new organisations to bring existing concessions directly under the Pleasure Beach umbrella, and between 1914 and 1921 the Rainbow Wheel, Scenic Railway, Canadian Toboggan Slide, Water Chute and the Captive Flying Machine were brought in-house by three new companies. The fact that the Scenic Railway and Water Chute were bought in after the financial failure of previous owners should remind us that operating amusement park rides, even in Blackpool, was not simply a licence to print money. The bankruptcy of the multiple concessionaire George Valentine Tonner in 1932 makes the same point. He had introduced the Dodgems to Blackpool, achieved national publicity for his spectacular Skee Ball final jackpot prizes, and held 15 Pleasure Beach concessions at his peak in 1926, although he seems to have frittered away a lot of his profits on implausible ventures outside Blackpool.[24]

After this interlude of financial consolidation, with novelties occurring at the level of sideshow rather than spectacle, three major and enduring new attractions appeared during 1922 and 1923, presaged by the introduction of the Whip, an American ride from Mangels of Coney Island, in 1920.[25] William H. Strickler reappeared in Blackpool, and worked successfully on the Noah's Ark and Virginia Reel, both of which opened in 1922, and the Big Dipper which opened in the August of the following year, two months

22 M.B. Rose (ed.), *The Lancashire Cotton Industry: a History Since 1700* (Preston, 1996).
23 Bennett, *Century of Fun*, p. 52.
24 Ibid., pp. 41–2.
25 Nick Laister, http://www.thegalloper.com/staticcontent/ukvinrides.html accessed 8 Aug. 2006. For the 1920 introduction date, Pleasure Beach Archives, Cuttings Books, 1920, p. 32, cutting from *Blackpool Times*, 21 July 1920.

**This comic postcard of the Whip was one of a series issued by the Pleasure Beach in 1925 for publicity purposes, featuring recent additions to the amusement park's menu of rides and focusing on their potential for generating laughter through embarrassment and gentle (or, in this case, not so gentle) sexual titillation. It was a long-lived ride, surviving until the reign of Amanda Thompson in 2005, by which time it had achieved iconic status for many amusement park enthusiasts.**

after the first of the Blackpool Carnivals.[26] As befitted Strickler's American origins and transatlantic career, these new attractions perpetuated the American influences on the Pleasure Beach's portfolio of pleasures. The Noah's Ark (not to be confused with the popular fairground carousel ride of the 1930s) was an American innovation of 1917, a fun house full of shifts and surprises on the complex journey between the model animals, as the boat rocked on its artificial summit of Mount Ararat and no foothold was ever secure, whether on stairway or stepping stone. The idea was sufficiently embedded in secular popular culture to form an acceptably slapstick version of a biblical story, and 'Old Noah' and his Ark featured on one of a series of cheerfully vulgar promotional postcards that the Pleasure Beach issued in the early 1920s.[27] The Virginia Reel also had American origins, but of an older vintage: Henry Elmer Riehl of New York had patented the

[26] J.K. Walton, 'Popular entertainment and public order: the Blackpool Carnivals of 1923–4', *Northern History* 34 (1998), pp. 170–88.

[27] Bennett, *Century of Fun*, pp. 44–5; http://www.themagiceye.co.uk ARKive Part 2, The Blackpool Ark, accessed 1 Aug. 2006.

**The Noah's Ark was an American import and the closest the Pleasure Beach went to adopting American-style biblical elements into its rides, although the dominant elements were comic and mock-frightening, as illustrated here. The animals here are those created by Walter Bernasconi in 1930. The artificial rock had its municipal counterparts in the 'rockification' of the promenade gardens on the North Shore during the 1920s. After undergoing a large number of further remakes and alterations over the years, Blackpool's Ark was one of only two attractions of its kind to remain operational in 2007.**

**The Virginia Reel, the third of the trio of new rides to be introduced in the early 1920s, proved long-lived and adaptable to changing tastes, as the scenery in which it was embedded could be refreshed without too much difficulty. It was the shortest-lived of the major new rides of this period, but it continued in operation for sixty years.**

**An aerial view of the Pleasure Beach in 1923, showing the new South Shore swimming baths and the beginnings of promenade extension work on the left. Boundaries were still unclear, and there was still little development to the south of Watson Road on the right of the picture. The Water Chute, Scenic Railway and Velvet Coaster stretch a long way to the east, and their vulnerability to the proposed extension of Bond Street through the Pleasure Beach is very clear. The Rainbow Wheel is still a prominent landmark.**

ride as early as 1907, and it was already in use at Coney Island's Luna Park in the following year, taking its name from that of Riehl's baby daughter, Luna Virginia, whose first forename came from the sister of the Park's owner, Skip Dundy, who in turn had given her own name to Luna Park itself. The Reel spun its passengers round as it twisted its way down a winding track through colourful constructed scenery, perhaps also conjuring up visions of the popular country dance of that name. It, too, featured on one of the promotional postcards, this time playing on male sexual anxieties as the whirling high-speed approach to a tunnel drew forth the worried comment, 'By gum! But we should make a mess if we missed this hole.'[28]

The Big Dipper was a much more impressive innovation. John Miller's invention of under-track friction wheels and rollers enabled faster speeds, tighter curves and steeper drops, and the introduction of the first Big Dipper in New Jersey in 1920 was closely followed by its adoption in Blackpool, after Bean had purchased the United Kingdom rights. It was emphatically another American development: Miller had begun his career

[28] Bennett, *Century of Fun*, pp. 45–6; http://www.themagiceye.co.uk/reel.html accessed 1 Aug. 2006.

working for LaMarcus A. Thompson, his business partner Harry Baker had worked with the Philadelphia Toboggan Company, and Strickler himself, who worked with them from 1917, had fronted the Federal Construction Company in Chicago. The name itself was taken from the American label for the constellation known in Britain as the Plough. This enduringly iconic ride, which provided spectacle as well as sensation and attracted spectators as well as riders, continued to earn its keep, like the Noah's Ark, into the twenty-first century. This was especially impressive as most of its American counterparts lasted for little more than five years, although the difficult times endured by the American amusement park industry from the mid 1920s must have contributed to this. But the longest-lived American Big Dipper lasted for only 54 years, as against 83 (and counting) for the Pleasure Beach version, although the latter was completely remodelled and rebuilt in 1936, with (inevitably) 'streamlined' cars. It replaced the switch-back railway of 1902 and added an exciting new accent to the fairground skyline, reaching 65 feet in height, with a maximum drop of 48 feet and a top speed of 60 miles per hour. It was also the Pleasure Beach's first one-shilling (5p) ride, but even in the darkening economic climate of the mid-1920s this was insufficient to deter the seekers after excitement who soon made it an enduring commercial success. The Big Dipper also found its way into the comic postcard series, imaginatively drawn and presented as a tonic for the jaded, featuring a high-kicking display of plump thighs and lacy underwear.[29]

After this flurry of activity, the amusement park novelties of the rest of the decade came from concessions rather than from the Pleasure Beach company itself, and were much less arresting than the Strickler developments of 1922-3. They included several small slides, rides and motor tracks, together with a second set of dodgem-style bumper cars under the label 'Autoskooter' or 'Autoscooter', although dodgems with effective steering and instant reversing were to be the invention of Lusse Brothers of Pennsylvania in 1928.[30] Bean himself brought in the Indian Temple of Mystery, playing to an enduring seaside interest in the exotically 'oriental', and an extensive boating lake, introduced in 1928. But it was Blackpool's local authority that continued to make the running in developing the resort

[29] Robert Preedy, 'Thrills in old age: 73 years of Dipper fun', at http://home.nyc.rr.com/johnmiller/bigdip.html accessed 1 Aug. 2006, provides a more convincing and circumstantial account than Bennett, *Century of Fun*, pp. 47–8. For the rebuilding, which generated a great deal of regional and national press publicity, Pleasure Beach Archives, Cuttings Books, 1935–6, pp. 35–6, 48–53.

[30] Seth Gussow, 'A short history of bumper cars', http://www.lusseautoscooters.com/history/html accessed 8 Aug. 2006.

as a whole, with the new swimming pool, the completion of the South Shore promenade, the Carnivals of 1923 and 1924, the landscaping and other improvements at North Shore, the creation of Stanley Park, and the return of the autumn Illuminations on an altogether novel scale, combining to overshadow the lesser achievements of private enterprise. The Pleasure Beach took care to advertise itself boldly along the southern railway approach to Blackpool, and in 1927 its name appeared as an official destination on the front of the Corporation trams. But when in 1926 TH Mawson, the distinguished landscape architect who worked on Blackpool's town planning scheme and provided some of the distinctive Beaux Arts/City Beautiful architecture for the Corporation's Stanley Park, prepared plans for a formal Pleasure Beach frontage in similar style, Bean did not take up this opportunity to enhance the image of a successful, respectable amusement park whose appearance still had more of the air of a random collection of disparate machinery than a modern, planned landscaped pleasure area.[31] But his commitment to respectability, which made for inclusiveness across cultures as well as classes, was never in doubt, as demonstrated by the Pleasure Beach's failure to open on Sundays (in contrast with, for example, the Kursaal at Southend) together with its commitment under his management 'not to permit gambling games of any kind', underlined by the perhaps self-interested statement that, 'All games on the Pleasure Beach have an element of skill', at a point when the Chief Constable was threatening to 'declare war' on gaming machines.[32]

By the later 1920s Bean seems to have been losing momentum, as the pace of innovation slackened and died away. The Pleasure Beach's financial results would not have borne out such a perception, as net annual profits grew from £18,784 in 1919 (itself a highly successful year) to £82,272 in 1929. Bean still paid his annual visit to the United States, where he was active in the National Association of Amusement Parks, and he was still highly visible in the local politics of Blackpool and sometimes on wider stages, as he became a vocal critic of existing conventions in local government. He had been raised to the dignity of Justice of the Peace in 1919 and to that of Alderman in 1925, suggesting a degree of acceptance among the local elite that overcame the negative consequences of his enduring antipathy for the powerful Tom Bickerstaffe of the Tower Company, despite the challenge the Pleasure Beach mounted to the dominance of the older town centre entertainment interests. By 1928 he chaired Blackpool's municipal

[31] Bennett, *Century of Fun*, pp.49–50, 52; Walton, *Blackpool*, Chapter 5; Helen Meller, *European Cities 1890s–1930s* (Chichester, 2001), Chapter 5.

[32] Pleasure Beach Archive, Cuttings Books, 1928–9, pp. 115, 124.

Finance Committee. His oratorical and analytical powers must have played a part, as must his involvement in Freemasonry, which was common currency among leading Conservative members of the Council, although he was always vocal in his condemnation of cliques and corruption. He was largely self-taught, but his cultural hinterland extended to membership of the local Dickens Fellowship and amateur operatic society as well as less intellectual pursuits like golf and bowls. His concern for managerial efficiency in urban governance, and for the reduction of local taxation, probably owed something to a perception that municipal initiatives in Blackpool were increasingly competing with, rather than complementing and supporting, the efforts of private enterprise, and specifically those of the Pleasure Beach. Seaside local authorities found themselves competing both for well-off residents (especially the retired, but also commuters) who were concerned about local taxation levels and had access to published comparative statistics; but they also had a competitive need to sustain a wider range of amenities and a more attractive environment than other towns, and it was important to generate positive publicity through stunts and events that might lose money in themselves but stimulate the wider resort economy. Bean's unwillingness to accept Corporation trading losses on the Carnivals of 1923 and 1924, which brought in magnificent publicity and huge numbers of visitors outside the main holiday season, despite a panic about alleged hooliganism on the second occasion, suggests that he thought the local authority was intervening too much in this regard. His successor would certainly share this view. Moreover, his last years were blighted by a difficult rearguard action against Corporation plans to drive a road through the Pleasure Beach from north to south along the Bond Street axis, crossing the existing Watson Road thoroughfare and cutting the Pleasure Beach into four, disrupting existing activities and complicating future plans. His premature death in January 1929 at sixty years of age, at the beginning of a cruise to South America and the Pacific, was unexpected and widely lamented; but it opened the way to a new Pleasure Beach regime that benefited from the relative stagnation of the late 1920s by having a free hand to move on to a new level of modernisation and sophistication during the following decade.[33]

[33] Bennett, *Century of Fun*, pp. 50–5; Walton, thesis, p. 512; J.K. Walton, 'Popular entertainment and public order: the Blackpool carnivals of 1923–4', *Northern History* 34 (1998), pp. 170–88. For the distinctive Conservative-dominated local politics of Blackpool, Walton, thesis, Chapter 9; Sam Davies and Bob Morley (eds.), *County Borough Election Results: England and Wales 1919–1938*, vol. 1 (Aldershot, 1999), chapter on Blackpool. For the role of local government at the seaside, Walton, *British Seaside*, Chapter 7, and N. Morgan and A. Pritchard, *Power and Politics at the Seaside* (Exeter, 1999).

The transition was difficult and took time. According to the star *Daily Express* journalist Hannen Swaffer, Bean left 'a larger fortune in America' to go with the £300,000 or so that was declared in England; but no succession plan was in place, and Bean had been both chairman and managing director of the Pleasure Beach.[34] Power was vested temporarily in the company secretary, Oscar Haworth, and the long-serving financial director, George Palmer, who was based in London. Bean's will left his controlling Pleasure Beach interests to his 25-year-old daughter Doris, recently married to her exact contemporary Leonard Thompson, an Oxford graduate in Natural Sciences who had spent time at the University of Wisconsin at Madison and at Uppsala University in Sweden, preparatory to starting a London-based career with the Swedish Match Company. On some assumptions this background might have looked incongruous in an amusement park proprietor; and Thompson, like his father-in-law, had enduring cultural interests, as expressed (for example) in a letter of 1960 to Brady McSwiggan of Pennsylvania's Kennywood park, apropos a recent Caribbean tour: 'The 10 days or so we spent in Yucatan were most absorbing as I have always found that the Maya and other pre-Columbian civilizations of the American Continent were of great interest.'[35] The Thompsons decided to take up the challenge, and began a dynastic succession that was to take the Pleasure Beach into the twenty-first century while rival concerns faltered and died. The interregnum while Thompson found his feet, and took an accountancy course to help him to understand the Pleasure Beach's finances, lasted only a few months, and by the end of 1929 he was taking over the reins as a director and company secretary, while Doris Thompson also became a director. An early decision, whose implications can only be guessed, was to replace Palmer's firm as the company's accountants; and the move to Kidson Taylor of Manchester helped to provide access to substantial loans from the city's District Bank. At a time of financial turbulence and unpredictability, as the Wall Street crash ushered in widespread and enduring trade depression, Thompson had plenty of other pressing issues to confront, not least the consolidation of ownership of the firm itself. It took two years to buy out the Outhwaite family, at a higher valuation than had been expected, a transaction for which the confidence of the District Bank was essential. There were also disturbing plans from a Leeds promoter for a 'World's Fair' on 142 acres at Squire's Gate, a short distance to the south, with a zoo, 'jungle', park and sports stadium, while the local authority's promo-

34 Pleasure Beach Archives, Cuttings Books, 1928–9, p. 114.

35 www.themagiceye.co.uk/id158.html, Leonard Thompson to Brady McSwiggan, 16 Mar. 1960, accessed 17 Aug. 2006

tion of an early season Pageant also threatened to compete for the Pleasure Beach's trade, as well as affecting attendances at afternoon shows in the town centre, although Oscar Haworth's comments to the local press were cautious and measured in their tone.[36]

By 1931 the Thompsons had secured their independence, and a greater degree of consolidated control than Bean had ever enjoyed. Meanwhile, they had also been dealing with Blackpool Corporation's plan to put the Bond Street road extension through the Pleasure Beach. The scheme had been incorporated into the 1913 agreement and the 1917 Improvement Act, reaffirmed in 1920–1 after discussions between the Corporation and the Pleasure Beach, but given a stay of execution until the beginning of 1932. Nevertheless, its existence had been an enduring distraction and irritant to Bean, despite his theoretically strong position as a long-serving Councillor, Alderman and committee chair. Thompson took up the cudgels with renewed vigour. The proposed route, extending Bond Street through the amusement park in a straight line, would involve the demolition and removal of the Scenic Railway, Velvet Coaster and Water Chute, at a cost that was publicly estimated (by the company) at £100,000. Opinion in the town was divided on the issue. Bond Street was South Shore's main shopping centre, and many traders hoped that the new road would put them in direct touch with affluent new residents of the housing development that was projected on municipal land behind the new promenade to the south of the Pleasure Beach. In late 1929, however, as discussions resumed between Thompson and his advisers and the municipal Town's Improvement Sub-Committee, the waters were muddied by proposals for an alternative road alignment that would follow the railway line along the park's eastern side and generate much less disruption, although the Water Chute would still have to go. Debate resolved itself into a struggle between the 'Straight Road Party' and the 'Crooked Road Party', and the Pleasure Beach began to gain ground. By November 1929 the *Gazette*, the most influential local paper, was arguing that the Pleasure Beach, as an asset to the whole of Blackpool, should come before the sectional interests of the South Shore traders, because it was South Shore's biggest single employer, one of Blackpool's largest ratepayers, and 'is conducted as well as any concern of its kind can be conducted.' This last might seem to be faint praise, but the Pleasure Beach was also 'a source of pride, just as the Tower, Winter Gardens, and similar concerns are a source of civic revenue and prosperity.' The Ratepayers' Association and the Trades Council held out for a straight road,

36 Bennett, *Century of Fun*, pp. 55–6; Pleasure Beach Archives, Cuttings Books, 1929–31, pp. 18, 38.

but in December a meeting of the South Shore Traders' Association itself voted by a narrow margin for the 'crooked road'.[37] This was still not the end of the story, but in January 1932, after continuing argument, a poll of Blackpool ratepayers voted by a ratio of five to one in favour of the less damaging alternative, and later in the year it was written into the new Blackpool Improvement Act. The Pleasure Beach's successful campaign was probably assisted by the change of management, as Thompson avoided Bean's legacy of conflict within the Council. His lack of direct involvement in municipal politics at this time may even have been an asset. The new route still meant the end for the Water Chute, and the removal (and updating) of the Velvet Coaster and Scenic Railway, but it was far less disruptive than the original proposal. This agreement cleared away the last problematic legacy of the Bean era and liberated Leonard Thompson to develop his own agenda free from inherited distractions. It had taken three years to reach this position.[38]

Even as Thompson began to find his feet in the business and to resolve his inherited problems, he was looking to the future. On his first visit to the United States on Pleasure Beach business, in 1929, he found an architect called Edward Schoeppe working for the Willow Grove amusement park in the Philadelphia suburbs. This was a classic American amusement park at the end of a street trolley line, and a big music venue, founded at the same time as the Pleasure Beach, but already beginning the long decline that eventually saw its replacement by shopping malls.[39] Schoeppe's beautification work must have been part of an attempt to stem decline, after the retreat of the street trolley company from running the park; but it impressed Thompson sufficiently to invite him over in 1931 to give some of the rides a modernist makeover, to improve the stalls facing Watson Road, and to design an ice cream stall of 1933 in a classic American diner style of the period, and a sea frontage to face the new promenade, which included a large News Theatre using a distinctive chevron or herringbone motif.[40]

Schoeppe's employment at the Pleasure Beach proved to be merely an earnest of intentions, however, and he seems to have returned to Philadelphia, where his firm, Alexander, Becker and Schoeppe, designed the enormous Art Deco Spanish Ballroom which opened in 1933 at the

[37] Pleasure Beach Archives, 1928–9 Cuttings Book, pp. 136–8, 149–50; 1929–31 Cuttings Book, pp. 3–4, 7, 10.

[38] Bennett, *Century of Fun*, pp. 57–8.

[39] http://www.wgpark.com accessed 5 Aug. 2006.

[40] Bennett, *Century of Fun*, p. 58, which refers to him as Scheppe, and information from Ted Lightbown. He is variously referred to in other sources as Edward and Edwin Schoeppe, assuming that the two architects are the same person.

Glen Echo amusement park in Maryland.[41] When between 1933 and 1939 Leonard Thompson set in motion 'the greatest programme of capital expansion in the history of the Pleasure Beach', his chosen architect came from closer to home. The reordering of the Pleasure Beach to adjust for the new road, and for the additional land on the seaward side that became available after the promenade works, provided a good opportunity for reorganisation, but Thompson was clearly set on pursuing his new vision as a matter of principle.[42] Joseph Emberton was a pioneer of modernist architecture in Britain, and 'one of Britain's most significant architects during the inter-war period.' He was identified with 'the beauty of simplicity', eschewing ornamental detail, and favoured steel and concrete tower blocks in a Le Corbusier idiom for future housing development. He also designed furniture and fittings to match the philosophy of his buildings. His commissions included work on the British Empire exhibition at Wembley in 1924, and the *Manchester Guardian* described him as 'the architect and designer of the new Olympia' at Kensington during 1929-30 (not to be confused with the opportunistic, and immediate, borrowing of the name by Blackpool's Winter Gardens). He also designed a distinctive clubhouse for the Royal Corinthian Yacht Club at Burnham-on-Crouch, Essex, in 1931. In 1933 he was in his mid-forties and at the peak of his powers, and even his commissions for retail premises were metropolitan and 'establishment' in tone. Significantly in the light of his later Pleasure Beach work, he had been selected to design the advertising exhibition at Olympia in 1927, 'the first such exhibition with a unified style'.[43] Thompson's awareness of such a figure, his willingness to engage him, and Emberton's positive response (he was to remain the Pleasure Beach's official architect until his death in 1956), speak volumes for the ambition, imagination and cultural reach of Thompson himself, and for the democratic optimism about the scope for linking modernist architecture and popular pleasures that was one of the positive features of a deeply contradictory decade.[44] Thompson took pride in his choice of architect, announcing on the occasion of a British Association visit in 1936 that, 'His work has been to present all these machines and devices in such a way that they look interesting to the English

41 www.cr.hpsgov/habs/absspan.htm accessed 13 Sept. 2006.

42 Bennett, *Century of Fun*, pp. 59–60.

43 Brighton University, Design History Archive, EMB19, *Manchester Guardian*, 30 Aug. 1934; ibid., unnumbered newspaper cuttings book, *Daily Mail*, 22 April 1929; *Cabinet Maker*, 20 July 1929; *Birmingham News*, 16 April 1932; Alan Powers, 'Joseph Emberton', *Oxford Dictionary of National Biography*; Rosemary Ind, *Emberton* (London, 1983).

44 Victoria and Albert Museum, 'Modernism: Designing a New World 1914–1939', 6 April to 23 July 2006, catalogue.

public, and at the same time to tie all these devices together by a certain continuity of architectural form, so that the place looks like an Amusement Park and not like a factory.'[45]

The initial contact seems to have come, prosaically, through Douglas Kidson of the Pleasure Beach's Manchester accountancy firm, who was aware of Emberton's work for another client, the multiple tailor Austin Reed, at his headquarters in London's Regent Street. But it led to a thoroughgoing change of design and image for Britain's greatest amusement park, in a way that ran parallel to the streamlined re-equipment of Blackpool's municipal tramway system during the same decade, after the arrival of Walter Luff as tramway manager in 1933. Streamlining was to be the great vogue of mid-1930s Blackpool: Thompson himself spoke in praise of it as a symbol of modernity when he returned from a 17,000 mile journey across the United States by air and streamlined train in 1935, and later in the year the *Blackpool Gazette* proudly (if implausibly) described the town as 'the streamlined resort'. But in the specific application of this appeal to all that was aesthetically and technologically modern, Blackpool was swimming successfully against the tide, as trams and amusement parks fell into decline or came under severe competitive pressure in other settings; and in the United States, especially, the two phenomena were directly connected, as the shift of urban transport from rail to road undermined the finances of amusement parks at the end of street trolley lines, and the number of active roller-coasters (a good indicator of the health of the amusement park industry as a whole) fell from 1300 in 1929 to around 200 in 1946. What was different in Blackpool was that the promenade tramway not only remained attractive and useful in its own right, but that the renewed investment it attracted from 1933 onwards provided a further boost to the continued popularity of the Pleasure Beach, without the necessity for giving over huge amounts of land for car parking. Cars and their owners might be worthy of rhetorical encouragement, but however people might arrive in Blackpool, it was more convenient for the Pleasure Beach, and better business for the Corporation, that they should make the journey to the amusement park itself by tram.[46]

Emberton began work at the Pleasure Beach rather tentatively in 1932, designing a station for the new miniature railway that marked the first step in Thompson's modernisation programme. Its replacement, after a fire two years later, was much more confident and distinctive in style. He soon

[45] Bennett, *Century of Fun*, p. 62.

[46] Ibid., p. 60; www.britishtramsonline.co.uk/survivalintro.doc accessed 6 Aug. 2006; Pleasure Beach Archives, Cuttings Books, 1935–6, pp. 3, 37.

developed his own clear vision of the overall project, telling the *Manchester Evening News* in 1934 that, 'We are gradually rebuilding the Pleasure Beach, keeping it in line with modern thought.'[47] Among other things, this meant a firm retreat from the common American practice of mixing the functional engineering of the roller coaster with booking offices and other ancillary buildings built to resemble a 'Moorish pavilion or Chinese pagoda': this kind of exotic ornamentation was completely out of place in the modern amusement park.[48] Emberton worked as part of a team, alongside the American roller-coaster designer Charlie Paige, as Thompson benefited from the ready availability of talent in an industry that was depressed elsewhere, as Blackpool and the Pleasure Beach defied the economic gloom of the early 1930s and exemplified the positive impact of falling prices on spending power alongside the growth of new consumer industries that also marked the decade.[49]

The American influence was further reinforced by the arrival at the end of 1933 of the roller-coaster designer Harry G. Traver, a refugee from bankruptcy while two of his formidable installations in the United States were closing down; and Thompson was also able to call on a team of artists to work alongside the amusement park technologists. They included the 'resident artist' Walter Bernasconi, a scenic artist by training who had been apprenticed to his father, a theatrical scene painter, and had worked for bazaars and international exhibitions before coming to the Pleasure Beach, where the output of his studio included the conversion of the Virginia Reel landscape into 'a copy of the Taj Mahal', the development in 1930 of a new (but short-lived) set of wood and cement animals with glowing eyes for the Noah's Ark, and the regular re-decoration of the Scenic Railway.[50] There was also the mural painter Margaret Blundell, whose work was later to appear (for example) on the Cunard luxury liner *Caronia*, which was launched in 1948, and (perhaps most impressive of all) the medal and coinage specialist Percy Metcalfe, whose animal designs had been used for the new Irish currency in 1928. He contributed subsequently to the design of coins for several other countries. Metcalfe also worked on medals for the British Empire Exhibition of 1924 and on the Jubilee coinage of 1935, and was to design the medal for the George Cross in 1940. In 1936 the London correspondent of the *Manchester Guardian* described him as an 'eminent and

47 Design History Archive, EMB19, *Manchester Evening News*, 31 Aug. 1934.

48 Design History Archive, EMB19, *Sunday Observer*, 2 Sept. 1934.

49 J. Stevenson and C. Cook, *Britain in the Depression: Society and Politics 1929–1939* (London, 1994); and for the underpinning of this section, Bennett, *Century of Fun*, pp. 61–9.

50 Pleasure Beach Archive, Cuttings Books, 1929–31, p. 33.

**At the Fun House the highbrow delights of Joseph Emberton's modernist architecture signposted the carefully planned craziness of the 'fun factory' interior, summing up the way in which the Pleasure Beach reconciled the calculating and the irrational to generate both enjoyment and profit. Its loss to a serious fire in 1991 was widely mourned by those who had experienced it, especially as adolescents. Here, however, the pleasure seekers of the 1930s are queueing for the Jack and Jill ride which adjoined the Fun House, warmly wrapped up on what looks like a bright but chilly spring day, but it is still noteworthy that almost all are adults, with just a sprinkling of children and adolescents.**

fastidious designer', just as Emberton was 'the most modernist of architects', while praising his 'ingeniously comical' new Noah's Ark animals, redesigned in a whimsical Cubist style. Among his Pleasure Beach activities was a contribution to a similar design for the entrance to the refurbished River Caves, and he was to produce an endless supply of costume designs for the ice shows in the new Ice Drome, for which the drawings survive in the Pleasure Beach archives. The Noah's Ark animals seem to have combined technological with artistic innovation: in 1952 Thompson sent Brady McSwiggan details of the Chrysaline process for constructing the external animals that succeeded Bernasconi's, which were 'built up in wire framing and covered with this Chrysaline sprayed from a gun. The Chrysaline is then painted with a transparent coloured paint', and each animal was lit

**The Pleasure Beach's crèche expressed the apparent paradox that it was eager to gain a reputation as a respectable and family-friendly attraction, while recognising that many of its rides were aimed at adults who would prefer to have their small children looked after elsewhere for the duration of the visit.**

from within at night using electric lamps. Metcalfe was still doing designs for Thompson in 1957.[51] It is surprisingly difficult to find out about the Pleasure Beach work of any of these artists except through sources related to the Pleasure Beach itself (the entry on Metcalfe in the *Oxford Dictionary of National Biography* makes no mention of it), suggesting that it neither found critical favour outside the Blackpool environment nor furthered their conventional artistic reputations. Thompson's ability to identify and make use of their talents is therefore all the more impressive.

In 1933 the team began work in earnest. Paige oversaw the installation of a new Roller Coaster, probably using recycled material from the Velvet Coaster, which had become a casualty of the Bond Street extension road. Emberton's contribution to this drew the comment from the *Manchester Guardian* that, 'With its 80-foot pylon-shaped tower, and its long fin-like

51 http://www.ultimaterollercoaster.com/coasters/history/design/history_traver.shtml and www.caronia2.info/ artour03.php both accessed 6 Aug. 2006; P. Attwood, 'Percy Metcalfe', *Oxford Dictionary of National Biography*; Pleasure Beach Archives, www.themagiceye.co.uk/id158.html Leonard Thompson to Brady McSwiggan, 25 Sept. 1952, accessed 17 Aug. 2006.

**The new station for the Roller Coaster was one of Joseph Emberton's first architectural contributions to the restyled Pleasure Beach of the 1930s, and set the tone for what was to come.**

planes, it must be regarded as an example of serious modern architecture enlivened by a few bold strokes of fancy.'[52] A year later the Fun House followed, on the site of the Water Chute's lake, thus replacing another attraction lost to road-building. Emberton's role was to design a capacious and excitingly lit envelope, complete with rocking letters, for 'the greatest Fun House in the world', an update of the Noah's Ark concept without the biblical referent and animal theme, offering a journey through destabilising and potentially embarrassing experiences such as rocking, dropping and shaking floors and a grating with a strong up-draught to lift the female victim's skirt. Some suggested that the frivolous nature of the contents might be logically incompatible with the stark functionalism of the architecture, but the *Manchester City News* was captivated nevertheless by its cosmopolitan modernity, claiming that the Fun House 'might come straight from Berlin', and adding that 'the interior is almost majestic in its stark beauty'. *The Architect* featured it in a portfolio piece.[53] It soon acquired a disturbing laughing clown figure near its entrance, after Thompson had observed its success in gathering a fascinated crowd during the Christmas

52 Design History Archive, EMB19, *Manchester Guardian*, 30 Aug. 1934.
53 Ibid., *Manchester City News*, 2 Feb. 1935; *The Building*, October 1934; EMB56, *The Architect*, 28 June 1935.

sales at the Galeries Lafayette in Paris, and bought it for the 1935 season at the Pleasure Beach, where it remained. Other amusement centres in Blackpool, such as the waxworks on Central Beach, were quick to copy it, and a member of the Mass-Observation team commented with distaste that these 'small hideous figures shaking with mechanical laughter' would 'bear looking into', as there was 'something peculiarly sinister and nerveracking *(sic)* about them.'[54]

Meanwhile, older landmarks such as the Rainbow Wheel and Helter Skelter were being abandoned, while Thompson's intensification of Bean's pursuit of a paying combination of respectability and security with wonderment and excitement was exemplified by his reaction to a claim by Harold Davidson, the former Rector of Stiffkey, that the Pleasure Beach had offered him a sideshow to exhibit himself after he had been driven off the 'Golden Mile'. Davidson was a former stage performer from a clerical family, a man with a colourful past who had been defrocked under highly contentious circumstances for alleged immoral conduct with London prostitutes, and had become the object of sustained media attention. In September 1932 he had been taken up by Luke Gannon, the leading 'Golden Mile' impresario of prurient and sensational shows featuring freaks and starving honeymoon couples, but the crowds at his exhibition of himself in a barrel, ostensibly to raise money to clear his name, were so disruptive that even the thick-skinned Gannon had to make his peace with the local authority. Thompson repudiated the suggestion that Davidson might find a home in a Pleasure Beach sideshow in the strongest possible terms, emphasizing the moral distance between Pleasure Beach and 'Golden Mile' that Bean had maintained, and underlining the incompatibility between Thompson's vision of a modern amusement park and the cheap, scruffy, disreputable stalls and arcades that dominated the Central Beach sea-front.[55] Thompson's concern for the Pleasure Beach's reputation, and that of his wife's family, had been made clear in the first months of his tenure, in June 1929, when he was abrasive, immediate and persistent in his repudiation of Pat Collins's claim that the Walsall showman had been on the verge of buying what became the Pleasure Beach site at the beginning of the century, only to lose out to a marginally higher last-minute offer from Bean after his agent was overheard bragging about the deal over a cigar in a hotel smoking room.[56] This was not the sort of reputation Thompson wished to endorse or perpetuate.

54 Mass-Observation Archive, W56/A, report of 31 June *(sic)* 1937, p. 19.

55 Bennett, *Century of Fun*, p. 59; Walton, *British Seaside*, pp. 109–10; Tom Cullen, *The Prostitutes' Padre* (London, 1975).

56 Pleasure Beach Archives, Cuttings Books, 1928–9, pp. 98–100.

**The Noah's Ark after its modernist makeover in 1937, complete with 'Cubist' animals by Percy Metcalfe, which attracted a great deal of attention.**

Thompson's re-making of the Pleasure Beach in the mid-1930s continued to emphasize clean lines, new materials and the respectability of modernity, always in alliance with the pursuit of business efficiency in giving the paying public what it wanted.[57] The new attraction of 1935, a very successful season, was the Grand National, a double roller coaster which offered the illusion of a race along parallel tracks and gave a ride of nearly two and a half minutes for a shilling (5p) while packing in over 2000 passengers (or £100) per hour. Emberton designed the station in what was becoming the new house style, and it acted as a magnet at the centre of the amusement park. The name, unusually, was resoundingly English (and also both northern and classless) as it conjured up the excitement of the premier steeplechase and popular betting event at Liverpool's Aintree racecourse. But the concept was American, borrowed and adapted from Traver's Cyclone at Long Beach, California. A year later, as the rhythm of innovation intensified, the Big Dipper was extended and made more exciting, although its capacity remained only two-thirds that of the Grand National; and again Emberton designed a suitably modernist station.[58] These were

57 Bennett, *Century of Fun*, p. 79.
58 For what follows Bennett, *Century of Fun*, pp. 65–70.

**The first of the two Eli Wheels of the later 1930s, essentially a fairground ride, nestles incongruously between the modernist pleasure architecture of Emberton (Grand National, left) and Schoeppe, on the right. The full car park is another sign of changing times.**

the emblematic new rides, but there were plenty of innovations elsewhere in the mid to late 1930s, such as the further restyling of the Noah's Ark and the introduction of a Maze. In 1936 the Ghost Train was reconstructed and expanded in the new style, after Harry Kamiya, the Japanese concessionaire who had brought it to the Pleasure Beach in 1930 as the Pretzel Ride (an alien concept to the British), had outgrown the constraints of the Pleasure Beach and moved on in 1932 to develop his own Luna Park on the 'Golden Mile', which featured an impressive array of classic freak shows including a human volcano, human pin-cushion and india-rubber man. He then multiplied concessions in other resorts and, in 1939, founded his own holiday camp just outside Morecambe. Here again, the change of name and theme (creating the first 'Ghost Train', after the name had been given currency by a play and a silent film during the 1920s) betokened the anglicisation of an imported idea.[59]

The Tumble Bug, Eli Wheel and Octopus, however, were essentially American fairground rides translated into the Pleasure Beach setting. The Tumble Bug was another import from the Pennsylvania amusement machinery industry, manufactured by Harry Traver's firm in Beaver Falls.[60]

59 www.butlinsmemories.com/2/id203.htm accessed 8 Aug. 2006; Pleasure Beach Archives, Cuttings Books, 1935–6, pp. 16, 47; and helpful clarification by Ted Lightbown.

60 Nick Laister http://www.thegalloper.com/staticcontent/ukvinrides.html accessed 8 Aug. 2006.

The Eli Wheel, a portable version of the 1893 Ferris Wheel which inspired it, was the brainchild of W.E. Sullivan of Roodhouse, Illinois, who built his first wheel in 1900 and incorporated the Eli Bridge Company to build the product commercially in 1906. The Eli Wheel was thus a long-established ride in the United States by the time it reached the Pleasure Beach in 1936; and although the wheels in question (a second one was quickly added to the first) were larger than usual, and offered a panoramic view of the park, this was not a dramatic innovation.[61] The Octopus of 1937 was much more state-of-the-art, and was to become a post-war fairground staple, especially in Ireland. It originated with the Eyerly Aircraft Company in Oregon, another American company with a misleading name, and was built under license in Blackpool by yet another American firm, Lusse Brothers of Pennsylvania, who fitted into the wider web of American influences on the Pleasure Beach by supplying roller-coaster parts to the Philadelphia Toboggan company, and had set up a factory on the Pleasure Beach to make Autoskooters and other amusement machinery for the European market, using British labour and materials and with Thompson as chair of the new company, in 1933.[62] Eyerly also patented the Dive-Bomber, a by-product of his background in flight simulators for the training of pilots, whose cars spun on their own axles from a vertical rotating arm. This ride, with its macabre name in the context of the times, has been described as 'fearsome' and the first true 'thrill ride', and it made its debut on the Pleasure Beach in 1939, also manufactured under license at Blackpool by Lusse.[63] The Moonrocket of the same year was another fairground ride, with origins in Germany (like a lot of fairground innovations of the dynamic 1930s), and taken up by the London fairground equipment manufacturer Lakin of Streatham. These additions to the Pleasure Beach menu lacked the distinctive flavour of the star rides, extending choice within the amusement park without offering anything outstanding to draw in visitors, and all readily transferable to travelling fairground use; but their initial lack of traditional fairground decoration and their relatively austere lines made them readily compatible with the Thompson and Emberton project.[64]

Two further projects of the later 1930s did add distinction and distinctiveness to the Pleasure Beach's offerings, as Thompson diversified into

61 http://www.history.illinois.org/frames/markers/22.htm accessed 8 Aug. 2006.

62 Gussow, 'Short history of bumper cars'; www.shef.ac.uk/nfa/history/rides/octopus.php accessed 8 Aug. 2006; Pleasure Beach Archives, Cuttings Books, 1935–6, p. 70.

63 http://nfa.dept.shef.ac.uk/history/rides/dive_bomber.php accessed 13 Aug. 2006.

64 http://www.thegalloper.com/backstories/0103lakin.html accessed 8 Aug. 2006; http://www.nfa.dept.shef.ac.uk/history/rides accessed 8 Aug. 2006.

**The Ice Drome extended the Thompson and Emberton modernist project in the direction of spectacular indoor entertainment of a kind rarely to be found elsewhere in Britain, which was capable of generating income throughout the year, plugging into Blackpool's reputation as a national centre of and innovator in live entertainment. The mural adds a touch of stylised light-hearted excitement. The crowd is visibly in transition, as bare-headed young men in open-necked shirts and women with knee-length skirts rub shoulders with the headgear and styles of an earlier generation.**

spectacular live entertainment and sophisticated catering. The Pleasure Beach had offered spectacle in crowded auditoria from an early state, not least through successive concessionaires offering the 'oriental' exotic in the Indian Temple of Mystery, the Chinese Theatre (under German management) and Gogia Pasha's 'Singhalese' devil dancers. In 1936 Thompson took this a step further by initiating the replacement of the ailing roller skating rink by an Ice Drome which would provide spectacular shows along with skating facilities for the paying public. Emberton designed a concrete and steel building with a capacity of 2000, and the first ice show was put on in June 1937, while in 1938 the Blackpool Seagulls ice hockey team began its career.[65] In the winter there were public skating sessions for the substantial local market, in a town whose resident population was now comfortably

[65] Peter Bennett, *Unrivalled Excellence: Hot Ice* (Blackpool, 1997), pp. 3–4.

**The Pleasure Beach as pleasure factory: an orderly crowd of the late 1930s queues, flows and eddies into little conversational groups. All ages from the teens upwards are present, with hardly any younger children and several single-sex parties of young people. Emberton's Fun House and Metcalfe's 'cubist' Noah's Ark animals are juxtaposed with older rides, including the Flying Machine. The modernist makeover is not yet complete.**

**The new Casino of 1939, at once the introduction to and climax of the Thompson and Emberton reinvention of the amusement park, seen from within the Pleasure Beach looking towards the north.**

**Taking tea in the Casino sun lounge just after the Second World War. There is an air of social pretension about the occupants of the wicker chairs and the bystanders, despite the animation visible on one or two expressive faces. This was not as democratic a space as Thompson sometimes liked to suggest.**

into six figures. Thompson was prepared to spend heavily on promoting the rink, hiring the poster designer Tom Purvis, famous for his posters for the London and North Eastern Railway's holiday destinations, to create 'Ice Drome Jack' at a time when he was receiving a very substantial £450 per year as a retainer from the railway company. Purvis, like Emberton, had worked for Austin Reed earlier in the decade, and also for the British Industries Fair, fitting into an established British recruitment pattern for the Thompson enterprise.[66] The Ice Drome was a most unusual amenity in a provincial town, even a major seaside resort, although Brighton had acquired one two years earlier; and the initiative again demonstrated Thompson's cultural hinterland and capacity to apply the lessons learned from his travels, in this case in both Switzerland (he was a winter sports enthusiast) and the United States.[67]

Even as the Ice Drome was coming into service, Thompson and Emberton began work on replacing the oriental Casino of 1913, which had marked out the entrance to the Pleasure Beach in what was then a conven-

66 www.ww2poster.co.uk/artists/Purvis.htm accessed 9 Aug. 2006.

67 Bennett, *Century of Fun*, pp. 77–9; http://www.mybrightonandhove.org.uk/ss_brightonhistory3.htm accessed 9 Aug. 2006.

tional idiom for expressing the exotic and exciting; but it had dated, certainly in the light of the Pleasure Beach's changing style and ethos, and its surroundings had outgrown it. It was, however, very strongly built, and the demolition team eventually had to resort to gelignite in order to remove it. Emberton's replacement building was an enormous concrete drum, with an Art Deco tower 92 feet high flaunting a dramatic external spiral staircase, all encased in white cladding shipped in by barge from the Netherlands. The Casino did not offer gambling, which was still unthinkable in a British setting: like its predecessor, its name evoked the imagined glamour and sophistication of the entertainment centres that formed the hub of polite society in the spas and seaside resorts of continental Europe. What it did provide was a grill room, an American soda bar, a restaurant with a French theme and a banqueting hall, while above it all were company offices and the chairman's flat. It was air conditioned and had automatic doors, using an 'electric eye' which had already been adopted on the Ghost Train in 1936 to activate the beheading of Mary Queen of Scots when an approaching carriage crossed the beam. The internal spiral staircase was every bit as dramatic as the external one, and Emberton's attention to detail extended to the full range of furnishings, as it had in the showpiece Pleasure Beach café with its Margaret Blundell murals. The *Manchester Guardian* was overwhelmed:'. . . this highly original building will be widely acclaimed, both as a signal vindication of functionalist theory and as a striking proof of the architect's incomparable skill in putting its precepts into practice.' But this was not to be reserved for the exclusive pleasure of an imagined elite among Blackpool's visiting public, increasingly plausible though this might seem as Blackpool began to attract metropolitan plaudits during the 1930s. It was supposed to provide accessible luxury for the 'masses', following a Blackpool tradition that dated back to William Holland's stewardship of the Winter Gardens in the 1880s, as parties from the mills and factories could arrive in bulk with all-in rail, meal and Pleasure Beach tickets by arrangement with the London, Midland and Scottish Railway. The relationship between Blackpool and the L.M.S. was closer than that with its predecessor the Lancashire and Yorkshire, and the railway's General Manager, the recently-ennobled Baron Stamp, who presided over the Casino's opening ceremony in May 1939, had already switched on the Illuminations (by remote control) in 1936, and on his visit to open the Casino was also made a Freeman of the Borough and named an express locomotive after the town. The L.M.S. recognised the importance of the holiday trade, as had also been witnessed by the opening of its Art Deco Midland Hotel, with artwork by Eric Gill, at Morecambe in 1933. This was also an area of interest for Thompson, as in 1938 he set up the Morecambe Pleasure Park Company, with himself as sole director, to run the amusement park that occupied an adjacent site on Morecambe promenade, close to one of the L.M.S. railway stations, and planned further development on land to be purchased from the railway company. He was also moving in on Southport's municipally-owned Pleasureland amusement park at this time, building in both cases on existing associations through his operating company Helters, which had also commissioned Emberton to work at Morecambe in 1936, although his design for a casino there was never built. The outbreak of war at the beginning of September interrupted the development of what could have been a very profitable set of relationships for the Pleasure Beach and associated enterprises.[68]

The level of Thompson's investment in remaking the Pleasure Beach helps to explain the degree of his hostility to the Council's pretensions to promoting its own entertainment menu in Stanley Park, in effective competition with private enterprise; but it also expressed his outright hostility to public enterprise in most forms. In 1935 he condemned the United States' National Recovery Act, with its extensive public works schemes, together with President Roosevelt's policies in general, as 'rank Socialism'.[69] In 1934 the Corporation was exploring the idea of a 'Wembley of the North' on the eastern side of the municipal airport at Stanley Park, incorporating the lake at Marton Mere, and including a motor racing track and a major entertainment building as well as a huge sports stadium.[70] This did not gather momentum, but in 1935 the Corporation's purchase of 462 acres of land in Lytham, just south of the borough boundary and dangerously close to the Pleasure Beach, to be 'developed for recreational purposes', provided a further basis for conflict.[71] The use of Stanley Park for Corporation fetes and other entertainments would have annoyed the Pleasure Beach management even without the longer-term threat of further municipal competition, and in 1936 Thompson closed the amusement park for four days in protest at the Corporation's extravagant Diamond Jubilee celebrations, arguing that they constituted unfair municipal competition for private enterprise which paid its local taxes, kept its

[68] Bennett, *Century of Fun*, pp. 79–85, 112; Walton, thesis, pp. 247–58, 317–18; J.K. Walton, 'Power, speed and glamour: the naming of express steam locomotives in inter–war Britain', *Journal of Transport History*, third series, 26 (2005), pp. 15–16; R. Pope, 'Railway companies and resort hotels between the wars', *Journal of Transport History*, third series, 22 (2001), pp. 62–73; Design History Archive, EMB54, *Manchester Guardian*, 27 Nov. 1936; *West Lancashire Evening Gazette*, 10 Sept. 1936; *Architects' Journal*, 17 Sept. 1936, p. 359; *Manchester Guardian*, 26 May 1939; EMB79, Casino plans.

[69] Pleasure Beach Archives, Cuttings Books, 1935–6, p. 3.

[70] Design History Archive, EMB19, *Evening Chronicle*, 31 Aug. 1934.

[71] Mass-Observation Archive, M56/D, Borough Treasurer to R.W. Glew, 1938.

entertainments going at a loss on the 'shoulder' of the season, and should not have to compete with subsidised municipal events on an inland site at a considerable distance from the town's commercial traders and amusement companies. The Corporation's plans for the second and third weeks in June, drawn up by its Attractions and Publicity Committee, included naval and military tournaments, a tournament of flowers, a Highland tournament, a motor rally and *concours d'élégance*, a national beauty contest, and a 'Feast of Orpheus', which was effectively a band contest. It also invited the Royal Lancashire Agricultural Society to hold its annual show, another major event, at Squire's Gate over August Bank Holiday week-end. This provoked Thompson into a public denunciation of the Committee's 'nonsensical' schemes, citing the failure of the previous year's 'Highland Flings' during the Scottish holiday period, and pointing out that the Corporation's newspaper advertising of the town would be cut to pay for staff salaries in the Attractions Department, while £1000 would go in subsidy to the agricultural show at the busiest point of the season. He argued that the Pleasure Beach spent more on billboard advertising than the Corporation, and that closing the amusement park for several days would hit the Corporation's gas, electricity and tramway revenues, put up to 1000 workers on the dole and deter visitors during the weeks in question. Robert Parker of the Tower Company gave 'wholehearted support' to Thompson's stance, and the next full meeting of the Council, amid lively scenes that culminated in a shouting match, set up an enquiry into the powers and duties of the Attractions and Publicity Committee. Shortly afterwards the popular magazine *Answers*, reporting on an interview with the Corporation's Publicity Manager, W.R. Foster, fuelled the flames by implying that the Corporation deserved the credit for recent improvements to the Tower, the piers and the Pleasure Beach itself. Thompson stuck to his guns, declaring that he was willing to co-operate with the Corporation to promote Blackpool as a whole, but would not accept direct competition from it subsidised by local taxation. The Pleasure Beach duly closed down for four days (but without putting a thousand people on the dole), attracting extensive publicity in the national popular press; and the chair of the Attractions and Publicity Committee, Alderman Ashton, commented darkly that this action 'would strengthen the hands of the Corporation if it ever sought wider powers in the future'. He continued hostilities by questioning the appropriateness of the Pleasure Beach to the development of the new Blackpool, and airing the idea of a new enclosure at the south end of the town to provide wholesome entertainment under municipal auspices. The actual festivities came close to confirming Thompson's worst predictions, making a substantial loss, as one day was washed out entirely, the largest crowds were estimated at no more than 5,000 and the total receipts at just over £1650. Most of the proposed processions were forbidden by the Watch Committee, which was one symptom among several of the divisions within the Corporation that this episode exposed.[72] The Stanley Park affair was a remarkable extension of the corporatist, interventionist Conservatism that was fashionable in some circles in the 1930s, but it was out of step with the Council majority at a time when Doris Thompson, whose role in the business side of the matrimonial partnership should never be underestimated, was becoming increasingly prominent in Blackpool Conservatism.[73] With hindsight, it seems clear that the threat of direct municipal competition was neither strong nor plausible, not least because the Pleasure Beach of the mid-1930s so obviously *was* in tune with the needs and expectations of a changing Blackpool. This was far from obvious at the time; but in the medium term Alderman Ashton's position was to prove untenable, and Thompson's intransigence won the day.

At this very time, the Pleasure Beach was gaining recognition both nationally and internationally for its striking combination of excitement, innovation and modernity, as some of the comments on individual rides and buildings have already shown. The trade press was highly supportive from the beginning. In August 1933 *World's Fair* praised recent improvements in the appearance of seaside amusement parks, as they became more permanent, more orderly, and more uniform in design, and used Emberton's appointment to illustrate 'the manner in which designers of the highest class are being called in to assist in making our parks more beautiful still'. Emberton himself had 'stated that while the Pleasure Beach was pre-eminent in Europe, it was intended to continue a gradual development, until it would be far beyond criticism, and stand alone as an architectural achievement of its type.'[74] In 1935, L. Edwin Fairest interviewed Thompson for *World's Fair*, arguing that, 'It would be difficult to see in what way his company's methods could be improved, as it employs experts in every phase, and in Mr Joseph Pemberton *(sic)* , the architect, they have one of the best specialists in the world. Every item is designed before it is made… even such things as railings and other subsidiary items have to conform in every way to the general scheme.'[75] The American trade journal *The Billboard* described Thompson in the same year as the 'King' of Blackpool.[76]

72 Pleasure Beach Archives, Cuttings Books, 1935–6, pp. 25–6, 69–70, 74–6, 81–2, 85, 87, 89, 91, 94–6.

73 For this paragraph see also Bennett, *Century of Fun*, pp. 70–1, 83–4.

74 Design History Archive, EMB19, *World's Fair*, 12 Aug. 1933.

75 Pleasure Beach Archives, Cuttings Books, 1935–6, p. 16.

76 Ibid., p. 29.

The visit of the British Association for the Advancement of Science to Blackpool in 1936, which owed much to the good offices of Stamp during the year of his presidency, included a visit to the Pleasure Beach 'to see how the masses are entertained', in Thompson's words, as part of a plan to made the British Association annual meetings more accessible and democratic, and provided excellent publicity as the media stimulated and responded to comments from the scientists. The tone of some of the publicity is captured by the *Daily Sketch* headline '2000 Savants Will Go Gay: Pleasure Beach Visit Planned'. Interviews with scientists provided enjoyable stereotypical copy: 'Professor Edridge Green, equipped with umbrella and raincoat and with his gold-rimmed glasses pressed firmly on his nose', was reported as enjoying his first experience of the Dodgems. Meanwhile, Frank C. Thomas gave a paper on 'The Psychology of Mass Entertainment', using the Pleasure Beach as an example of the exploitation of 'the fear-escape propensity', and Thompson himself spoke to the engineering section on the importance of American technology in the international development of amusement park rides.[77]

Meanwhile the Pleasure Beach had become a regular setting for popular films, including versions of Stanley Houghton's controversial drama *Hindle Wakes*, and the Gracie Fields vehicle *Sing As We Go*, which drew crowds of onlookers for the filming of the scenes. The film historian Andrew Higson describes Blackpool as 'the heart of the film', with the Pleasure Beach 'literally at the centre – it takes us just over half an hour to get there, and when we leave, there are another thirty minutes of the film left...' This was magnificent publicity. The Pleasure Beach team supplied and managed attractions for international exhibitions in Brussels and Paris, and Thompson attracted publicity by chartering a large Imperial Airways airliner to take a Blackpool party (including the Corporation's Director of Publicity) from Squire's Gate airport to the Brussels venue. Meanwhile, Thompson became increasingly a name to conjure with in the United States, as the Pleasure Beach continued to develop while the American amusement parks struggled. In 1937 the *Sunday Times*, commenting on the Pleasure Beach's role in exporting engineering management to the Brussels and Paris exhibitions, asserted that it was ahead of Coney Island in the export of 'engineering know-how.'[78] A year later, *The Scotsman* argued that the wheel had now turned full circle, as the amusement proprietors both of Atlantic City and of

[77] Ibid., pp. 53, 126, 128–9; Design History Archive, EMB54, *West Lancashire Evening Gazette*, 10 Sept. 1936.

[78] Andrew Higson, *Waving the Flag: Constructing a National Cinema in Britain* (Oxford: Clarendon, 1995), p. 150; Design History Archive, EMB54, *Sunday Times*, 15 Aug. 1937.

continental Europe took their cue from pilgrimages to the Pleasure Beach: 'Blackpool leads the entertainment world, as Paris leads the world of fashion.' Unlike some other comments on the Pleasure Beach, there was some substance behind these observations, as the Blackpool amusement park went from strength to strength while the Coney Island parks themselves began their long decline, though under very different circumstances.[79] Emberton's own family holiday visit to the United States in 1938, using the *Queen Mary* in both directions, included trips to Coney Island and Atlantic City; but the surviving home movie footage suggests that he took a greater interest in skyscrapers and the quirks of American business culture than in fairground architecture, although the brief Coney Island section includes a Dive-Bomber in operation before the ride had reached Blackpool.[80] Coney Island was still worth a visit, but Emberton had nothing to learn from it, and the Pleasure Beach was now setting the international pace.

The Pleasure Beach was certainly becoming visible enough to attract a great deal of comment from outside Blackpool, most of it favourable. At the very beginning of the Thompson regime, Hannen Swaffer described the Pleasure Beach as having 'all the joys of Coney Island, packed in one small space.'[81] In a more academic idiom, Wesley Dougill of the Department of Civic Design at Liverpool University praised the amusement park a few years later as 'an example of seemly layout of what had formerly been an unsightly agglomeration of shanties.'[82] William Holt, the eccentric Lancashire novelist and essayist of the 1930s, writing on 'The North on Holiday' for Manchester's *Daily Dispatch* in 1934 (before the important innovations of the second half of the decade and at the very beginning of the modernist makeover), was fascinated by the popularity of the Pleasure Beach's dedication to 'fun that makes you scream' in ever-changing forms: 'Mysterious inventors have been at work secretly in their laboratories, and as a result of their clandestine labours yells and shrieks of terror echo over the Irish Sea.' He interviewed Leonard Thompson and his management team, 'the general staff of this vast army of mirth makers, the leaders of this perpetual campaign against the dumps', and was suitably impressed by the sheer scale of the Pleasure Beach's operations, with an 'executive staff of over a hundred, and a further 1,000 employees' at 'the greatest concern of

79 Bennett, *Century of Fun*, pp. 74–7; Pleasure Beach Archives, photographs of filming of *Sing As We Go*, 1934; Cuttings Books, 1935–6, pp. 25, 29; Cross and Walton, *Playful Crowd*, Chapter 4.

80 Screen Archive South East, Brighton, Joseph Emberton films, 'American Visit', ID No. 1565.

81 Pleasure Beach Archives, Cuttings Books, 1928–9, p. 114.

82 Pleasure Beach Archives, Cuttings Books, 1935–6, p. 22.

its kind in the world', which used (among many other things) forty tons of paint per year. Thompson emphasized that this was a family business whose success was based on personal attention to detail, and chose to highlight the Pleasure Beach's unique 'system of accountancy', as 'the biggest *coin* business in the country. We have a copper machine which counts the coppers and makes them up in 5s (25p) bags. The money is shovelled into the machine like coal. We have machines behind the scenes which even bankers have not got.' There were, in fact, four counting machines, two for copper and two for silver, which were indeed 'state of the art' in the mid-1930s. This was, above all, a business based entirely on hard cash, with no cheques or credit. According to Swaffer it employed 90 cashiers in 1929. After some prompting, Thompson explained that most of the 'terrifying gadgets in the fun houses', as Holt put it, were now designed in-house and manufactured 'in our machine works', which another journalist described as being a hive of activity behind the scenes in the winter of 1935-6, including scientific innovations involving luminous paint and 'invisible rays operating queer and alarming animals.' Holt also gave credit to the 'expert architects' the firm employed, giving special mention to Emberton's new Fun House. This was all very matter of fact, but it did not prevent Holt from concluding with a romantic reference to 'the happy crowds which were circulating in this brightly-painted wonder world with its intense whites in the sunlight.' Holt was capable of responding sceptically to Corporation propaganda, and of insisting elsewhere that Blackpool really belonged to its visitors; but this report endorses the idea that the Pleasure Beach was genuinely in tune with their needs and desires, and that while its core business was still with Lancashire working people, it was capable of attracting all classes, a verdict that would be music to Thompson's ears.[83]

This was a view from Blackpool's own heartland: Holt was based in Todmorden, on the Lancashire/Yorkshire border, and knew whereof he spoke. But his perceptions were in keeping with the fashionable metropolitan critic James Laver's optimistic view of the Pleasure Beach's essential innocence, at about the same time:[84]

> A Pleasure Beach is a wonderful institution, full of every kind of harmless amusement that the brain of man can devise... How simple are human pleasures, after all! To hurtle down a slippery slope on a doormat,

[83] William Holt, 'Merry Mirth-Makers at Blackpool', *Daily Dispatch*, 4 Aug. 1934, p. 6; Pleasure Beach Archives, Cuttings Books, 1935–6, pp. 2, 35.

[84] James Laver, 'Blackpool', in Y. Cloud (ed.), *Beside the Seaside* (London, 1938, first edition 1934), pp. 170–2.

> to rise in the air on a flying machine firmly tethered to its central pin, to ride a horse, or a bird, or a dragon, round and round for ever to the sound of music which fatigues no musician for it is all produced by a steam-engine… to angle for goldfish… to eat ice-cream and toffee-apples – does not this list contain within itself, as it were in miniature, the sum total of possible human pleasures? The Pleasure Beach is Monte Carlo without its greed, the Scenic Railway the Alps without the fatigue of going there, the joys of *gourmandise* without their expense, the Cresta Run without its danger. It is the final solution of the periodical need for an orgy, a safety-valve for the high spirits of mankind, set in a scene of extraordinary beauty, made doubly beautiful when night falls and the flares are lighted, and little rows of fairy lights hang on strings from booth to booth, and all along the perilous convolutions of the aerial railway.

Nothing could have been better calculated to gladden the heart of the Pleasure Beach management, especially as nothing controversial was intended by the use of the word 'orgy'. Here was a fulsome endorsement of their promotion of cleanliness, modernity, security and the attraction of a more up-market crowd, indeed a seamless amalgam of the classes which set potential conflict to one side, and whose message continued to be widely endorsed through the rest of the decade.

The international gossip columnist Charles Graves, brother of the poet Robert, thought the Pleasure Beach (like Blackpool in general) might prove too much for some effete metropolitan constitutions: 'My own final memory was of the one Londoner I knew whom I met on the Pleasure Beach. It was four o'clock in the afternoon. But already he was dazed. He opened his mouth to say something. A gust of laughter from a dozen merry mill-girls and their escorts drowned it. He gave up trying, and slunk away. Blackpool is no place for weaklings.'[85] This was before the new regime of Thompson and Emberton had transformed the Pleasure Beach from a pleasure factory, a description that gains credence from surviving photographs in which some of the amusement machinery is reminiscent of colliery winding gear, to a 'modern amusement park', which by 1937 was opening on Sunday, joining a trend which had been promoted assiduously by South Coast resorts earlier in the decade.[86] In the latter guise, it was capable of entrancing the prolific, assiduously self-promoting writer and popular journalist Beverley Nichols, who declared that 'Blackpool Pleasure

85 Charles Graves, *–And the Greeks* (London, 1930), p. 191.
86 Mass-Observation Archive, W56/F, Sunday 5 Sept. 1937.

Beach has Coney Island beaten to a frazzle. Blackpool is gayer, more brilliant, and oh how much cheaper. And in that Pleasure Beach are buildings of real beauty…'[87] Not that these were completely original perceptions: in 1933, at the very beginning of the Emberton regime, Gordon Beckles had told readers of the *Daily Express* that the Pleasure Beach 'knocks Coney Island into a cocked hat because it is so beautifully conceived and honestly constructed.'[88] A Mass-Observation report at Easter 1938 noted that the Pleasure Beach was a defining landmark on the train journey round the coast to Blackpool, 'with its many struts, gleaming white because they have been newly painted for the season… The peak of the big plunge of the Big Dipper, decorated by Emberton with a conical top that looks like a Tartar's hat, the golden globe with coiling serpents round it pivoted on the point, is the focus of all eyes.'[89] The observer expected his readers to know who Emberton was. In the summer of 1940 another member of the Mass-Observation team was even more laudatory: 'As distinct from the usual fairs this seemed clean and refreshing – the effect of the white concrete, the paved ground, the neat decorations, the brilliant paint on the side shows, and the lack of rasping music from "merrygorounds"…'[90] Blackpool had long attracted celebratory comment, sometimes with patronising undertones, for its sheer energy and working-class vitality. For a London socialite with aesthetic pretensions to praise the architecture and décor of the Pleasure Beach, and to compare it favourably, as Nichols did, with European resorts as well as with Coney Island, was a significant step further. So was praise from the self-consciously anthropological Mass-Observers, who were usually suspicious of 'slick' commercial entertainment. Thompson's re-making of the Pleasure Beach had clearly been an immense success. But the onset of the Second World War meant that difficult times lay ahead.

87 Quoted by Bennett, *Century of Fun*, p. 70.
88 Design History Archive, EMB19, *Daily Express*, 31 Aug. 1933.
89 Mass-Observation Archive, W56/C, description of train journey from Bolton to Blackpool, Easter 1938.
90 Ibid., W56/B, 'A day in Blackpool', 5 Aug. 1940.

# 4 The Post-War Pleasure Beach: New Challenges, New Initiatives

**Another aerial view of the Pleasure Beach, this time in the 1940s, after the Thompson and Emberton restyling, the new road, the promenade extension and the other changes of the inter-war years. The layout and boundaries appear much more formal and clearly defined than was the case in 1923.**

As in August 1914, the outbreak of the Second World War interrupted a bumper holiday season, although in this case the frenetic climax of enjoyment and investment during the last summer of peace was partly due to recognition of the imminence of the conflict, and the shutdown in Blackpool was immediate and unquestioned. There was much more advance warning in 1939 than a quarter of a century earlier, and a better understanding of an enhanced potential for death, destruction and disruption, especially for civilians. As in the previous war, however, Blackpool was in a position to benefit from the closure of competitors on the south and east coasts (with the exception of Brighton) and the renewed misfortunes of the Isle of Man. It also gained from the presence of a year-round population of several thousand evacuated civil servants, together with troops in training (especially for the Royal Air Force), and munitions workers, especially those who assembled Wellington bombers at the enormous aircraft factory at Squire's Gate. About a million troops passed through Blackpool during the war, with up to 50,000 in town each week, many of whom had never been there before (and many of whom, like the present writer's father, were to return there on honeymoon and then with their families).[1] By July 1940 the Wakes holidays had resumed, after a hiatus during the mid-year crisis of the Dunkirk evacuation and the fall of France. At August Bank Holiday week-end 78 coaches left Blackpool for Manchester alone with returning holidaymakers between 6 and 11 pm on the Sunday, and the railways were also busy. The Tower Company paid a handsome 15 per cent dividend at the end of 1940. The subsequent arrival of free-spending American troops later in the war, to join (for example) the Poles who were already noticeable in August 1940, together with Blackpool's surprising freedom from enemy bombing raids, set the seal on what may have been the most prosperous years in Blackpool's history, as the boom in local property prices corroborated.[2]

The Pleasure Beach shared in this prosperity to the full. It remained open throughout the war, and indeed throughout the year, providing regular dances and even ice shows alongside the amusement park attractions, despite the shortage of male dancers, and playing its part in sustaining military and civilian morale.[3] At August Bank Holiday in 1940 Mass-Observation recorded that it still looked 'practically the same as prewar to the outward eye', despite the regular passage of low-flying RAF bombers overhead and a vogue for brightly-coloured RAF forage caps for holiday wear. There were 'no special "war" attractions', to the surprise of the observer, who noted a lack of 'the usual boisterous spirit' and of 'a sense of freedom and irresponsibility' among 'a good crowd', but it was business as usual.[4] Problems had to be surmounted as the war dragged on, especially in the form of labour shortages, and the maintenance backlog that accumulated through constant usage and shortages of materials was storing up additional difficulties for the post-war period; but comparatively the Pleasure Beach fared as well during the war as did Blackpool as a whole. Across the Ribble estuary at Southport, for example, Pleasureland was requisitioned for military use between early 1941 and July 1944, and for the

1 E. Walton, *From Hepthorne Lane to Rangoon… and Back* (Shirland: Higham Press, 2006), pp. 47, 53.

2 Walton, *Blackpool Landlady*, pp. 187–8; Mass-Observation Archive, W56/B, 'A day in Blackpool', 5 August 1940.

3 Bennett, *Hot Ice*, pp. 10–15.

4 Mass-Observation Archive, W56/B.

next two seasons only a quarter of the park was open for business. It was not until 1946 that complete reopening took place here. In contrast, the Pleasure Beach was ready to welcome the pent-up demand for controlled excitement and commercial enjoyment from the hordes of post-war holidaymakers who came pouring into Blackpool in the immediate post-war seasons, as the British seaside benefited (along with, for example, cinema and professional spectator sports) from a combination of full employment and a lack of competing spending opportunities in a period of rationing, austerity and shortages of consumer goods. Although, for similar reasons, it was to be unable to innovate or expand its offerings for more than a decade, it was available to play its part to the full in the resurgence of the popular holiday industry.[5]

In 1951 the Lancashire and Merseyside Industrial Development Association reported on the post-war prospects of the Lancashire coast. It was optimistic about the future of 'the holiday industry', although the most recent employment figures, for 1947, showed that employment in entertainment, sport, catering and accommodation had still to return to its 1939 level. The research team stressed the continuing attractiveness of the area's natural advantages, commenting that, 'Nor is there any indication that the limits of development have now been reached. On the contrary, with the coming of less austere days one can look forward to a time when visits to the seaside will become even more frequent and more widespread...'[6] This spare, formal, administrative prose reflected the official thought of the time, which assumed that the delayed implementation of the Holidays with Pay legislation of 1938 would unleash a post-war flood of new holidaymakers on to popular coastlines, straining existing facilities to the limit and threatening to swamp the natural beauties of the shore in a welter of ugly new development. These hopes and fears were exaggerated, especially in the case of Blackpool. The Holidays with Pay Act was a cautious and limited measure that brought paid holidays to the cotton industry for the first time, but made little difference to other industries. After all, the popular Blackpool holiday industry was already well established long before the Second World War, while by the 1940s the Fylde coastline was almost completely built up and there was little room for Blackpool to expand within its present boundaries.[7] Blackpool's visiting public did continue to grow in numbers during

5 Bennett, *Century of Fun*, pp. 88–9; S. Copnall, *Pleasureland Memories* (St Albans, 2005), pp. 43–6.

6 Lancashire and Merseyside Industrial Development Association, *The Lancashire Coast* Area (Manchester, 1951), pp. 28, 32.

7 Barton, *Working-Class Organisations and Popular Tourism*, Chapter 7.

the post-war generation, but this owed more to full employment, rising spending power and the town's capacity to generate publicity and sustain its unique live entertainment programme than to the pre-war legislation, although the continuing expansion of holiday entitlements through the 1950s and 1960s also played its part.[8]

The crucial changes of the post-war generation as they affected the Pleasure Beach were the opening out of the seaside holiday for the first time to a broad spectrum of working-class families with young children, in a period of full employment, incomes outpacing inflation, and from the early 1950s a rapid expansion in consumer choices and personal mobility; and the gulf that opened out between the generations from the mid-1950s as the first cohort of teenagers with their own distinctive fashions, tastes, music and entertainment began to break up the conventions of the family holiday, although this happened later in Blackpool than it did in London's immediate orbit.[9] In any case, it took time for these developments to work their way through, especially the emergence of a separate teenage culture; and the immediate post-war years featured continued rationing, housing shortages and limited access to consumer goods, pushing people to seek outlets for their spare cash in sport and entertainment, and benefiting those aspects of resort economies while generating record attendances at professional football, cricket and speedway matches. Blackpool did well out of this, while lacking in either the resources or the incentive to redevelop or modernise its menu of entertainments and attractions, at a point where future preferences were becoming increasingly difficult to forecast, and remaining vulnerable to subsequent changes in popular taste and fashion; and at first the Pleasure Beach was also slow to innovate, not least because essential raw materials and labour were still expensive and in short supply.[10]

It was not until the late 1960s that Blackpool began to feel the heat of competition from new destinations for the main summer holiday, at first involving new coastlines, destinations and kinds of holiday within Britain (especially caravan, camping and touring holidays, as more and more working-class families began to acquire cars, and the opening out of destinations in Devon and Cornwall) to a greater extent than the exotic Mediterranean package destinations that remained a minority and overwhelmingly

8 Walton, *British Seaside*, pp. 61–4.

9 Ibid. p. 137; J.O. Springhall, *Youth, Popular Culture and Moral Panics* (Basingstoke, 1998).

10 I. Zweiniger-Bargielskowa, *Austerity in Britain: Rationing, Controls and Consumption 1939–1955* (Oxford, 2000); M. Hilton, *Consumerism in Twentieth-Century Britain* (Cambridge, 2003); Walton, *Blackpool*, Chapter 6.

middle-class taste until the end of the decade.[11] Photographs of the central Promenade and beach on sunny days in the summers of the 1960s show tightly packed crowds occupying every available square metre, and give an impression of continuing prosperity, even as the cotton industry on which all this had been founded was going into its death throes, the Wakes holiday system began its decline into extinction and the Central railway station, the main point of entry for East Lancashire holidaymakers for nearly a century, closed its doors for the last time in 1964. Buses and coaches were a different matter, as was the extension of the motorway system to provide ever-easier access by road. In 1967 the journalist Graham Turner detected some unease about the future, even as Blackpool continued to pull in the crowds. Municipal proposals in the mid-1960s for 'a redevelopment of the central area which would include a casino, elevated walkways and skyscraper hotels' came to nothing, not least because of fear of alienating existing customers; and nor did an ambitious plan for a domed hotel in the round and exhibition hall on the Central Station site, which was intended to evoke the Taj Mahal. Turner noted the continuing invisibility of teenagers – the Mods and Rockers disturbances of 1964 had not touched Blackpool – and an overriding commitment to conservatism and respectability. Many of the visitors, in fact, had a 'period look about them. There are the same elderly men in brown suits and black shoes, the same pale and bloated toddlers being bawled out by their fathers... The town seems to be run by and for the over-forties and the under-fourteens.' Contemporary photographs largely bear out this assessment, although there was some evidence of challenging teenage demeanour on the beach and Golden Mile, and even on the Pleasure Beach itself. Turner remained optimistic, noting a variety of new developments and emergent entrepreneurs; but Blackpool's future direction, torn between tradition and innovation, seemed uncertain, and it was during this decade that national press reports began to look for and seek to illustrate evidence of incipient decline, sometimes using photographs of empty Pleasure Beach rides to make their point. More frequently, however, the Pleasure Beach was highlighted as an exception to the general unease of 'Blackpool at the crossroads', although the company's secretive accounting practices as a very private limited company made it difficult to back up the impression that it was going 'from strength to strength', as was suggested in 1971.[12]

11 J. Demetriadi, 'The golden years', in G. Shaw and A. Williams (eds.), *The Rise and Fall of British Coastal Resorts* (London, 1997).

12 Turner, *North Country*, pp. 133–7; Pleasure Beach Archives, Cuttings Books, 1953–69, *Bolton Evening News*, 2 July 1968; *Daily Telegraph*, 7 Aug. 1967; 1969–74, *Sunday Times*, 24 Oct. 1971; *Manchester Daily Telegraph*, 22 June 1972; Alfred Gregory, *Blackpool: a Celebration of the 1960s* (London, 2003).

A year later the Corporation was uneasy enough to commission its first professional visitor survey, and the results were alarming enough to provoke changes in policy. The profiles for age and social class were both disturbing: half the visitors sampled were over 45 and one-third of them were unskilled manual workers and state pensioners, while the overwhelming majority of the rest were manual workers. A very high proportion of those surveyed, especially the day-trippers, were multiple repeat visitors. The dangers of failing to make an impact beyond a loyal but ageing existing clientele or to recruit the next generation, and of failing to retain the best-paying visitors, were only too apparent; and this was before the proliferation of cheap airborne package holidays to Mediterranean destinations really began to make inroads into the working-class holiday market. This was more a development of the 1980s than the 1960s. But Blackpool responded to the challenge with remarkable success, at a time when other old-established popular resorts in Scotland and Northern England, especially, saw sharp declines in their holiday businesses, as the impact of overseas and domestic competition was sharpened by the rapid development of commercial entertainment in the cities from which visitors were drawn, the widespread failure to update attractions and accommodation and the closure of many established entertainments as fashions changed and old industrial markets fell away, and the loss of that sense of distinctiveness and adventure that had been a hallmark of the seaside. Growing awareness of the pollution of beaches and bathing water also made an impact, and among the most serious casualties of this combination of adverse influences were several of Blackpool's neighbours and rivals, especially New Brighton, Morecambe and Douglas.[13] To some extent the decline of competing resorts was undoubtedly a result of Blackpool's own success, as new attractions during the 1970s and 1980s (most obviously the Zoo and then the new Sandcastle leisure pool complex which replaced the South Shore baths) helped to reverse the incipient decline and recover significant numbers of middle-class and better-off working-class families in younger age-ranges, if only for second holidays, no doubt drawing visitors away from less dynamic rivals with less clearly-defined identities. By the time of the next major visitor survey, in 1987, the profile had been refreshed, the problems for the time being surmounted or pushed aside. Here Blackpool is usually assumed to have been bucking a national trend, though recent research on seaside economies in the last thirty years of the twentieth century suggests that most were doing better than is usually assumed, with positive local employ-

13 Walton, *Blackpool*, Chapter 6; J. Urry, 'Cultural change and contemporary holiday-making', *Theory, Culture and Society* 5 (1988), pp. 35–55.

ment and migration trends even in the tourist industries. Blackpool shared in these optimistic trends, but comparatively it lay close to the bottom of league tables of economic performance, job creation and attractiveness to migrants among the 43 largest seaside resorts in Britain. But at the turn of the century extensive investment in sea defences and bathing water purification, involving funding from the European Union and the privatised utilities, together with long overdue embellishment of the promenade with artwork and street furniture, helped to sustain the tourist industry.[14]

The new Blackpool developments involved joint ventures between local government and external organisations, and a sequence of dubious decisions and outcomes during the 1980s, including the early financial problems of the Sandcastle, wrested credibility from the Council in spite of the improving visitor numbers and profile, as the Conservatives lost political control to Labour for the first time after more than a century of local government domination. Meanwhile a series of takeovers and mergers took the established local entertainment industry definitively out of Blackpool hands, a process that was already in motion during the 1960s, while it struggled to adjust to the entertainment revolution of the late twentieth century.[15] The 'Golden Mile' had been redeveloped from the late 1960s, losing some but not all of its distinctive raffish allure, while the late Victorian Grand Theatre, a Frank Matcham masterpiece, had been successfully rescued from bingo and demolition by a group of local activists and resurrected as a live theatre. The season shifted from the old summer Wakes period in July and August, with the decline of the cotton industry and of old industrial holidays more generally, to focus on the Illuminations, and on week-ends and short breaks spread through most of the year, rather than main summer holidays. New niche markets developed, involving gay tourism attracted by kitsch and camp aspects of Blackpool's historic reputation and by the developing gay night-club scene, led by Basil Newby, a local entrepreneur in an older Blackpool tradition, and his 'Funny Girls' revue which eventually took over the enormous Art Deco Odeon cinema near the main surviving railway station. Pubs and clubs also attracted the new market in 'stag and hen' parties, although the alcoholic excess and public lewdness associated with the development of this aspect of the 'evening economy' proved off-putting to the more traditional visiting publics when their paths crossed. But it was not until the end of the twentieth century that this cocktail of contradictions threatened to shake itself apart, as visitor numbers fell into sudden decline and a sense of crisis began

14 C. Beatty and S. Fothergill, *The Seaside Economy* (Sheffield, 2003).

15 Pleasure Beach Archive, Cuttings Books, 1953–69, *Financial Times*, 23 May 1969.

to permeate the resort. Between 1987 and 2003 official calculations of visitor numbers per year fell from 13.2 to 10.6 million, but to make matters much worse average length of stay fell from 5 to 2.4 days and visitor spending from £800 million to £500 million per year.[16] During the 1990s serious problems of poverty and social dislocation were becoming increasingly apparent in some of the older boarding-house areas close to the town centre, in association with drug abuse and anti-social behaviour, especially where traditional working-class visitors had given way to benefit claimants living in bed-sit accommodation. By 2004, on one measure, Blackpool was Britain's 24th most deprived local authority, having lost 40 per cent of its holiday accommodation units over the previous twelve years, most of which had been converted into houses in multiple occupancy.[17] At the beginning of the new millennium the town found itself in transition, looking for an injection of income streams from casino gambling to fund a massively ambitious plan for urban renewal, while at the same time looking to its entertainment heritage and historic built environment to develop a heritage tourism policy that included a campaign for designation as a UNESCO World Heritage Site under the new 'cultural landscape' rubric.[18]

The Pleasure Beach, after a slow post-war start, became increasingly important to Blackpool as a whole, as a distinctive pole of innovation and enterprise with an enduringly successful record of pulling in the crowds. As a family business which kept renewing itself with hands-on family management into the third and then the fourth generation, defying the conventional Lancashire wisdom of 'clogs to clogs in three generations', it increasingly stood out from the corporate leisure capitalism that came to dominate the other big entertainment businesses, culminating in Leisure Parcs' dominance of most of the Blackpool entertainment industry through its ownership of the Tower, the Winter Gardens, the three piers, Louis Tussaud's, the Sea-Life Centre and several smaller venues. In a Blackpool entertainment industry which was increasingly more complementary than competitive, as most visitors came to sample a range of enjoyments rather than choosing exclusively between them, the Pleasure Beach's high national and (increasingly) international profile played an increasingly important part in sustaining the popularity of the resort as a whole. Without the Pleasure Beach, post-war Blackpool would have found it more and

16 Office of the Deputy Prime Minister, Select Committee on Coastal Towns, 2006, written evidence, Blackpool Council, p. 146.

17 For this paragraph in general, Walton, *Blackpool*, Chapters 6–7; and for these statistics, ODPM, 2006, p. 147.

18 John K. Walton and Jason Wood, 'World Heritage Seaside', *British Archaeology* 90 (2006), pp. 10–15.

more difficult, over time, to remain buoyant and competitive in an increasingly challenging environment. But this is a complex story which deserves detailed examination, beginning with what now seems to be the very distant world of the post-war transition.

For several years after the war, the Pleasure Beach's reputation outran a reality which was slow to return to the spirit of innovation and modernity that dominated the 1930s. A Ward, Lock *Red Guide* of the early 1950s was describing the Pleasure Beach of 1939, glossing over the fact that it was gradually recovering from war and austerity and searching with desperate ingenuity for materials to make the most basic of repairs and redecoration, when it rhapsodised about the amusement park's 'evolution into the super, streamlined fun centre that it is today' as 'one of Blackpool's greatest romances', emphasizing the importance of the early Coney Island links through W.G. Bean and underlining the park's centrality to the town's holiday identity: '…thousands say it would be no Blackpool holiday without a thrilling ride on the "Big Dipper".'[19] Blackpool had got off lightly during the war itself, especially by comparison with southern resorts such as Margate, but it shared to the full in the problems of post-war adjustment, under circumstances where government priorities were directed at stimulating coal production and promoting manufacturing industries aimed at export markets which could improve the balance of payments. Domestic holidaymaking and the entertainment industry met none of these criteria, although they provided rest, recreation and an outlet for consumer spending for the workers in those industries.[20]

The return to normality was gradual and belated. The municipal Illuminations had recommenced in 1949, anticipated a year earlier (only eighteen months after the fuel and power shortages of the devastating winter of 1947) by the Pleasure Beach's own electrical display.[21] But although Thompson recommenced his annual visit to the United States in 1947, exchange controls made it impossible for him to convert his hard cash into dollars on a sufficient scale to do serious business (buying roulette chips on transatlantic liners and exchanging them for dollars did not generate enough liquidity for the purchases he needed), and he loaned out some of his surplus cash to help his friend Austin Reed, the multiple tailor, through his own seasonal problems. The Pleasure Beach had money, but for several years it was unable to spend it: labour as well as material was in short

19 Ward, Lock and Co., *Guide to Blackpool* (n.d., c. 1951), p. 50.

20 E. Brunner, *Holiday Making and the Holiday Trades* (Oxford, 1945); Barton, *Working-Class Organisations and Popular Tourism*, p. 191.

21 T. Regan and A. Hazlehurst, *From Lamp to Laser* (St Albans, 2004), p. 72; Alex J. Robertson, *The Bleak Midwinter* (Manchester, 1987).

**One of the first rides to receive a makeover after the Second World War, as austerity eventually retreated from the mid 1950s onwards, was the River Caves, whose Central American Aztec or Mayan theme may have owed something to Leonard Thompson's interest in the pre-Columbian archaeology of the Yucatan peninsula.**

supply, and in 1951 even the showpiece metropolitan Festival of Britain site had to be very sparing in its use of timber.[22] A few years later, in 1961, when Blackpool's *Official Holiday Journal* described the Pleasure Beach as 'the capital of fun and the centre of gay adventure, where you may experience the excitement of flying through the air or travel on water and land with laughter and exciting surprises at every stage of your journey... this wonderland is thronged with thrill and mirth-provoking rides,' the post-war resumption of investment and innovation had only just got under way.[23] It came too late for Joseph Emberton to play a full part: he died suddenly in 1956, after designing a remarkable, geometric, almost brutalist tower for the Ghost Train in 1954, which had to be demolished in 1961. He was also probably the architect of the Penny Arcade of 1955, whose Festival of Britain style embellishments likewise suggested a move away from the unified style of the 1930s, although the Mayan or Aztec treatment given to the River Caves in 1954 may have owed more to Thompson's own interest in pre-Columbian civilisations.[24]

22 Bennett, *Century of Fun*, pp. 90–1; John Ratcliff, 'Architects and the Festival of Britain', in M. Banham and B. Hillier (eds.), *A Tonic to the Nation: the Festival of Britain 1951* (London, 1976), p. 111.

23 County Borough of Blackpool, *The Official Holiday Journal* (Blackpool, 1961).

24 Pleasure Beach Archive, photographic collections, and information from Ted Lightbown.

**The Haunted Swing was the first new ride of the post-war period, and although it was neither a novelty nor a high profile attraction there were always interested consumers of its challenges to perception and equilibrium.**

Emberton's successor, John Ratcliff, was also well connected with, and acted as a link between, the worlds of contemporary architecture and exhibitions. He remained proud of his roles as deputy director of architecture and deputy controller of construction at the exhibition site of the controversial Festival of Britain on London's South Bank in 1951, and he was to design the British pavilion at Expo '58 in Brussels, the first post-war international exposition, just as Emberton had involved himself in work for international expositions, sometimes under Pleasure Beach auspices.[25] But opportunities for architectural and design work remained limited for several years, and Emberton's remained the dominant influence on the Pleasure Beach's architectural appearance.

The first new shoots of post-war innovation in the mid-1950s were tentative and small in scale: television aerials sprouting on Noah's Ark, and the

[25] Ratcliff, 'Architects and the Festival of Britain', pp. 110–12. Bennett, *Century of Fun*, pp. 91, 94, mistakenly refers to him variously as Jack Radcliffe or Ratcliffe.

conversion of the aeroplanes on the Captive Flying Machine into rockets to meet the new imaginaries of the space age.[26] The first new ride after the war, the Haunted Swing, was introduced in 1954, but had its origins in fairground illusion rides of (probably) the late Victorian period. These early versions formed the subject of a scientific article published in 1895. The ride consisted of 'a platform on which an individual sits or stands and then experiences considerable self-motion although little physical movement occurs. The visible room surrounding the person is not anchored to the ground, but rotates around them', as the swing appeared to go over the bar from which it hung, introducing sensations of giddiness and nausea. A group of scientists interested in visual perception tried out the Pleasure Beach version in the early twenty-first century, finding that it failed to produce the full sensation of swinging over the bar although, on the credit side, no-one was physically incapacitated by exposure to it. So it was neither a new idea, nor a full equivalent of earlier travelling fairground rides, although its longevity at the Pleasure Beach suggested success in pulling in the punters. As one scientific commentator pointed out, it was in a sense an extension of the principle of the rotating chair or centrifugal swing, used therapeutically in the treatment of insanity from the early nineteenth century, and appreciated as an enjoyment by the 'idiots', in the terminology of the time, at whom it was directed. From being imposed on patients as an extreme (though eventually addictive) form of therapy, such abnormal motion became a sought-after feature of Victorian fairground rides; and the Haunted Swing might be viewed as a particularly direct application of this principle, perhaps also building on the way in which 'fairground phenomena' might 'embody an understanding of illusions... far in advance of the contemporary visual science'. But it was not exactly an original addition to the Pleasure Beach's post-war menu of attractions.[27]

By 1957 an easier commercial climate and the relaxation of restrictions on currency exchange made it possible to buy in the first new American rides, at a time when the transatlantic amusement park industry was continuing its sustained decline. The Hurricane and the Sky Ride were less than spectacular, but at least they offered something different; and they inaugurated a period of intensive innovation which kept the Pleasure Beach in pole position among British amusement parks in a period of accelerating and potentially threatening change in entertainment and pop-

[26] Bennett, *Century of Fun*, p. 91.

[27] N.J. Wade and P. Hughes, 'Guest editorial', *Perception* 31 (2002), pp. 1159–64; N.J. Wade, 'The original spin-doctors: the meeting of perception and insanity', *Perception* 34 (2005), pp. 253–60.

**The Derby Racer of 1959 also adapted and extended an earlier concept for Pleasure Beach use, but in this case the combination of craftsmanship, lighting effects, scale, speed and ingenuity of design made for an enduringly successful addition to the amusement park's bill of fare, as well as a dramatic view from above and a striking contrast with the Flying Machine.**

ular culture.[28] Soon afterwards the first major new rides of the post-war period, the Derby Racer and Wild Mouse, were both constructed in-house by Pleasure Beach staff. The Derby Racer stands as a tribute to the technical and artistic skills that were available on site, as well as marking one of John Ratcliff's most important architectural contributions. It was an accelerated carousel ride, almost a 'white-knuckle' version of the concept, in which the horses moved backwards and forwards as well as up and down, giving the illusion that they were racing, and reaching speeds of up to 25 miles per hour in the outside file. The idea was American in origins and dated from 1917, and the template was borrowed from Toronto's Sunnyside Park, where a similar carousel had operated between 1924 and 1955. Frank Wright, the Pleasure Beach's General Manager, supervised the carving of the 56 wooden horses and the highly complex arrangements of cables and gearing that made them work; and the whole device took two years to build. Ratcliff's role was to design a light alloy dome with a diameter of 119 feet to house the new ride in fitting splendour, and the roof was enhanced with more than a thousand electric bulbs. This hybrid between fairground

[28] Bennett, *Century of Fun*, p. 94.

art and architectural modernism marked the Pleasure Beach's renewed commitment to innovation and excitement, although (as so often) it adapted a well-established ride for British consumption rather than introducing something entirely new.[29] Meanwhile, in 1958, the Wild Mouse also began operating. This unassuming roller-coaster, with its tiny 'soap box' cars adorned with mouse faces and whiskers, provided a lively (some said rough) ride in a small compass and became very popular with enthusiasts. In this case the idea came from Germany, where several manufacturers were producing examples by the mid-1950s, and Blackpool's adoption of the ride came just two years after its first appearance at a United States amusement park. Construction in-house was unusual, but Palisades Park in the United States had done the same thing a year earlier, and the success of this venture underlined the skills and versatility of the Pleasure Beach's workforce, although the responsibility for the construction of big new rides subsequently reverted to outside firms. The Wild Mouse proved to be the last of the Pleasure Beach's wooden roller-coasters, and within a year the American firm Arrow was building the Matterhorn, with a tubular all-steel track, for Disneyland at Anaheim, California. The challenge of Disney, and of the new kind of theme park that it represented, was to be a theme of the second half of the twentieth century.[30]

Meanwhile the Pleasure Beach took the opportunity to adopt an exciting and still exotic new transport technology to unite the northern and southern halves of the park, which was still divided in the middle by a public road, while providing a bird's-eye view of the Pleasure Beach and its surroundings. In 1961 it installed an Alpine-style chair-lift. The immediate impetus seems to have come from the installation at the Brussels Expo in 1958, where Thompson's son Geoffrey was working, boosted by Thompson's own enthusiasm for winter sports. But this was part of a widespread vogue for chair-lifts at this time, and Butlin's were already operating a similar structure (as a 'rope railway') at their Skegness holiday camp in 1959, the first of six, while the emerging rival theme park at Alton Towers, in Staffordshire, had one by 1963. Where the Pleasure Beach scored was in the claim to authenticity that the use of the Swiss Von Roll chair-lift system might provide, as opposed to the British technology that was adopted elsewhere, with the exception of Butlin's at Barry Island; but this was a limited

[29] Ibid., pp. 94–5; Nick Laister, http://www.thegalloper.com/backstories/0303derby.html accessed 13 Aug. 2006; http://www.ridezone.com/rides/derbyracer/ accessed 13 Aug. 2006.

[30] http://www.s104638357.websitehome.co.uk/html/wildmouse_main.htm accessed 13 Aug. 2006; http://www.personal.psu.edu/faculty/v/a/vac3/wdm.html accessed 13 Aug. 2006; Cross and Walton, *Playful Crowd*, Chapter 5.

**The present writer remembers the introduction of the Monorail as an exciting futuristic novelty, and a good way of getting a view of the park and of the other rides from unexpected angles, when it was introduced in 1966. In this view it is juxtaposed very effectively with the Eli Wheel, a giant clown figure and a double-deck Blackpool tram.**

claim to distinction.[31] In July 1966 a further aerial internal transport system was installed, this time taking the form of a monorail. Again there was a Swiss connection, through its use at the exposition of 1964 in Lausanne, where it had demonstrated its ability to weave effectively through a congested environment. Butlin's at Skegness were ahead of the Pleasure Beach, opening their monorail as early as 1965, but the Blackpool version laid claim to being 'England's first commercial monorail system'.[32]

As popular purchasing power and consumption continued to expand during the 1960s, the pace of innovation and investment at the Pleasure Beach gathered momentum, as it had to in the light of increasingly lively and sophisticated competition. There were recurrent threats of new rivals within Blackpool, as a consortium of showmen and media executives looked at the possibility of setting up a British version of a Disney theme park in Blackpool in the early 1960s, while Billy Butlin, who had already

31 Bennett, *Century of Fun*, p.95; http://www.butlinsmemories.com/chairlifts.htm accessed 13 Aug. 2006.

32 Bennett, *Century of Fun*, p. 97; http://www.butlinsmemories.com/monorails.htm accessed 13 Aug. 2006; Pleasure Beach Archive, Cuttings Books, 1953–69, *Blackpool Gazette*, 29 July 1966.

**Alice's Wonderland made an unusual connection between the Pleasure Beach and Disney, and the link with an established character and story line of fiction and fantasy also marked a departure, which was not to be repeated, from the usual Pleasure Beach philosophy of 'the ride's the thing'. The castellation is a slightly unexpected motif. The March Hares build on a Pleasure Beach tradition of fantasy animals, but the young woman wearing a swimsuit on dry land, and with a cowboy hat slung round her shoulders, is a novel sight that Leonard Thompson might not have appreciated.**

shown his ability to steal a march on the Pleasure Beach by introducing new rides at his holiday camps, showed interest in a Blackpool venture in 1962. This must have concentrated Thompson's mind.[33] At the start of the 1960s Arrow Engineering, founded in Mountain View, California in 1946 and later established in Clearfield, Utah as Arrow Dynamics, began a long commercial relationship with the Pleasure Beach even as it continued to work for Disney, its first big customer. It supplied the Turnpike, described by Nick Laister as 'an elevated concrete car track... looking rather like a multi-storey car park', a race track ride which fitted in with the rapid growth of popular motoring at this time, and whose American name was eventually changed to the Grand Prix; and Alice's Wonderland, a 'dark ride' through the Lewis Carroll fantasy world built under license from Disney, an unusual

[33] Cross and Walton, *Playful Crowd*, pp. 206–8; Bennett, *Century of Fun*, p. 96; Pleasure Beach Archive, Cuttings Books, 1953–69, *West Lancashire Evening Gazette*, 3 Sept. 1962.

**The Log Flume was a particularly attractive new ride, taking existing American technology further than before and breaking records for cost and length when it was introduced for the 1967 season. Its demise in 2006 was widely mourned among contributors to amusement park websites.**

collaboration that must have arisen through Arrow's contacts with the Disney empire.[34] Disney executives visited the Pleasure Beach as part of their programme of investigation for the development of Disneyland, which opened in 1955 and which Thompson inspected in his turn in 1957; but the peculiar blend of sanitised nostalgia and synthetic excitement associated with the Disney theme park (as opposed to, for example, the Disney film) proved difficult to export from the United States, although the remaking of the Pleasure Beach in the 1930s under Thompson and Emberton anticipated aspects of the Disney agenda, which was to become very attractive to British tourists in Florida and, eventually, in northern France, towards the end of the twentieth century.[35] A third new attraction at the beginning of the 'sixties, the Paratrooper, was essentially a fairground ride, an update of the post-war Spitfire, promoted by the manufacturing company Ameco in 1960 with the promise that only 12 would be made. The Pleasure Beach took the first one and placed it on the site formerly occupied by the Dive-Bomber as a like for like replacement, but like the

[34] http://www.thegalloper.com/backstories/0103blackpool.html accessed 14 Aug. 2006.
[35] Bennett, *Century of Fun*, pp. 94–5; Cross and Walton, *Playful Crowd*, pp. 206–9.

**The Astroswirl of 1969 continued the flow of increasingly ambitious new installations that marked out the late 1960s and early 1970s, forming a distinctive local landmark on the Pleasure Beach skyline when seen from the Promenade, but here seen at a distinctive angle from below and within.**

other rides that were capable of being toured by fairground operators it was a supplementary rather than a stand-out attraction.[36]

In 1962 Thompson sought to impose some coherent shape and direction on this piecemeal development by adopting a five-year investment plan, budgeted at half a million pounds. This involved uniting the Pleasure Beach site by building a broad concrete bridge across Watson Road, where traffic through the middle of the park was an increasing hazard, and transforming the Casino with newly themed bars and restaurants, offering cabaret and dancing. The Watson Road proposal generated some interesting debate, exposing enduring divisions on the local authority, as councillors divided almost equally in 1963 over whether the Pleasure Beach was an essential asset and source of innovation and revenue which should be allowed to go its own way, or whether it should be viewed with suspicion as wanting 'something for nothing' and trying to manipulate the Council.[37] But it was not until the end of this period of consolidation and updating, in 1967, that

36 http://www.nfa.dept.shef.ac.uk/history/rides/paratrooper.php accessed 14 Aug. 2006.

37 Pleasure Beach Archive, Cuttings Books, 1953–69, *West Lancashire Evening Gazette*, 8 Aug. 1963; Bennett, *Century of Fun*, pp. 96–7.

the next really spectacular new thrill ride was inaugurated. The Log Flume, another Arrow product, was a genuinely new development, although it evolved from earlier water-chute rides. It was first introduced in 1963, as El Serradero, in the Spanish section of the American Six Flags park; but Blackpool's was the first in Britain and the longest anywhere, installed at a cost of £180,000 that put previous ventures in the shade. It marked the beginning of a sequence of high-profile and well-publicised new installations, signalling a new level of innovative activity in the Pleasure Beach's development.[38]

The sequence of new rides that spanned the late 1960s and early 1970s, helping Blackpool as a whole through a difficult period, continued the established mixture of origins. The excitingly-advertised Monster of 1968, the first to be installed outside North America, was in principle an update of the Captive Flying Machine with additional dimensions of movement, and came directly from Expo '67 in Montreal, where Thompson purchased it outright.[39] This international exposition also provided the inspiration for 'Europe's largest acrylic dome', the Perspex-clad hemisphere 70 feet in diameter that housed the Astroswirl of 1969 and allowed John Ratcliff to make another significant contribution to the Pleasure Beach's skyline and architecture; but the ride itself, using rapid rotation and centrifugal force and manufactured by Hrubetz of Salem, Oregon, was a version of their prototype Meteorite of 1958 and was to become widespread as a fairground ride from the mid-1970s.[40] The in-house rebuilding of the Pleasure Beach Express, with a nostalgic Edwardian theme, refreshed a perennial, gentle and popular attraction. The most impressive new ride, however, was the Gold Mine of 1971, a 'dark ride' which made its own impact on the skyline of the park. It was installed by Pleasure Beach staff under the supervision of Arrow, whose concept it was, and the cost was again well into six figures at £150,000. The romantic story that the ride's designer, the Hollywood special effects expert Maurice Ayers, had won an Academy Award for the parting of the Red Sea in Cecil B. DeMille's *Ten Commandments* of 1956, cannot be substantiated in full. Ayers's sole (shared) Academy Award had been in 1948, for his part in the development of a lightweight plaster process for set construction, and the special effects Oscar for the film in question went to

38 Bennett, *Century of Fun*, pp. 98–9; http://www.parktimes.com/sections/spain/flume.htm accessed 17 Aug. 2006.

39 Pleasure Beach Archive, Cuttings Books, 1953–69, *Blackpool Gazette*, 27 July 1968; Bennett, *Century of Fun*, pp. 100–1.

40 http://www.nfa.dept.shef.ac.uk/history/rides/meteorite.php accessed 19 Aug. 2006; Pleasure Beach Archive, Cuttings Books, 1953–69, *Plastics and Rubber Weekly*, 23 May 1969.

John Fulton. But the ride itself attracted a lot of attention and proved an enduring success.[41]

The big roller coasters remained crucial to the Pleasure Beach's appeal, with Easter week receipts from 1973 suggesting that the takings for the three ran neck and neck, with the Roller Coaster at £3328 slightly ahead of the Grand National and Big Dipper. Management resorted to ingenious ways of trying to enhance their profitability. In 1973-4 the Pleasure Beach sought exemption from Value Added Tax for tickets on the coaster rides, arguing that the Big Dipper was a device for the transport of passengers, like a railway, rather than an entertainment. At the Court of Queen's Bench this claim elicited a legal definition of a Big Dipper from Lord Widgery and colleagues: 'Like a confused spiral staircase, the track crossed and recrossed *(sic)* itself and made spirals up and down thereby producing gradients and corners which gave the passengers an exaggerated idea of the speed at which they were travelling and the dangers of the journey.' But this was not calculated to sustain the Pleasure Beach's case for the Big Dipper as means of public transport, which was eventually lost.[42]

Meanwhile the Ice Drome had continued to form an important part of the Pleasure Beach's empire, linking it to the evolving tradition of spectacular live entertainment that was central to Blackpool's holiday industry as a whole. A state of the art lighting system was installed as early as 1946, and towards the end of the war the artistic, 'high culture' aspirations of the enterprise were underlined by the commissioning of Dame Laura Knight, then known more for her circus and ballet paintings than for her landscapes, to paint an Ice Drome scene for exhibition at the Royal Academy. The post-war shows were strongly themed, lavishly costumed and generously staffed, with a *corps de ballet* to supplement the skaters, and (in 1952) a total of 95 artistes. The vigorous response to severe fire damage in the summer of 1949, which brought the Ice Drome back into use in little more than five weeks at a time of serious shortages of labour and materials, was a logistical triumph, especially as it coincided with the development of a second ice theatre at the Morecambe park, although this was housed more prosaically in an aircraft hangar. The crisis also brought Frank Wright to the Pleasure Beach for what turned into a thirty-five year career which culminated as General Manager. The sheer number of performers involved in the ice spectaculars seems to have been unsustainable as wage bills rose – the Pleasure Beach's official historian describes it as 'Leonard Thompson's

41 http://www.themagiceye.co.uk/id139.html accessed 19 Aug. 2006.

42 Pleasure Beach Archive, Cuttings Books, 1969–74, Daily Telegraph, 8 Aug. 1973; *Daily Mail*, 8 Sept. 1973; *All England Law Reports*, 26 Mar. 1974, pp. 1011–14.

greatest extravagance' – and by 1957 the number of artistes had fallen to 55, 26 of whom formed the *corps de ballet*. This was still a remarkable number for a predominantly working-class provincial resort, even one with current aspirations to be the national capital of popular entertainment; and the dancers formed part of what was, by 1956, one of only two permanent ice shows in Britain, the other one being at Bournemouth. During the 1960s the cast was steadily reduced, while the Morecambe show was abandoned in 1962 and the Blackpool Christmas pantomime ceased in 1959. Efforts were made to bridge the growing gap in tastes and preferences between the generations, as new trends in popular music were incorporated while an older style of visual spectacular was retained. Television, often perceived as a competitor, provided a new boost in the early 1970s through the popularity of its screenings of world skating championships, whose British winners could be tempted to the Blackpool shows even as leading conventional entertainers became too expensive; but in the mid-1970s a further transition was getting under way, with simplified stage machinery, the sale of thousands of stored costumes in 1974, and the abandonment of ballet. This was to be continued under the new regime after Leonard Thompson's death in 1976.[43]

The rhythm of innovation in the amusement park was sustained through the difficult inflationary years of the mid-1970s, with the Tom Sawyer raft ride of 1973, which had affinities with the early Disneyland experience of Tom Sawyer's Island, and was unusual in lasting a full quarter of an hour; and the much more exciting Space Tower of 1974, again inspired by the international exposition at Lausanne in Switzerland ten years previously. This ride, featuring a revolving viewing platform which rose and fell around a pillar 158 feet in height, provided another strong new accent on the Pleasure Beach skyline. It was another major new investment; and at the same time, the Captive Flying Machine, after seventy years' service at the Pleasure Beach, was given a full reconditioning and a vote of confidence in its future. This marked the beginning of the distinctive Pleasure Beach commitment to keeping the most iconic of its older rides in service alongside the new ones so long as they were earning their keep, celebrating and making use of its own history as an additional attraction and marketing ploy, just as Pennsylvania's Kennywood was doing. This was to become a significant aspect of the Pleasure Beach's attractiveness, especially to the growing international fraternity of enthusiasts for roller coasters and other amusement park rides, during the late twentieth century. Thompson seems to have been

[43] Bennett, *Hot Ice*, pp. 14–48; Dame Laura Knight, *Oxford Dictionary of National Biography*; Pleasure Beach Archive, Cuttings Books, 1953–69, *Evening Post*, 12 Jan. 1974.

developing an interest in preservation and display at this point, acquiring a collection of vintage cars and an early Caterpillar ride from 1924; but any plans to take this further were pre-empted by his death in September 1976, which was unexpected but came after a prolonged period of ill health.[44]

As with the premature demise of William Bean, the Pleasure Beach management had made no contingency plans for continuity of succession in the event of Thompson's death or inability to carry on working; but they were fortunate that Thompson's son Geoffrey quickly rose to the occasion to carry on the succession, at forty years of age. Born in 1936, at the height of his father's modernist re-invention of the Pleasure Beach, he had a public school education at Shrewsbury (his parents had attended Manchester Grammar School and Malvern Ladies' College) and followed a degree in Economics at Christ's College, Cambridge with a business administration course at the University of Pennsylvania's Wharton Business School. This was located in the heart of what has been described as the 'fertile crescent' of amusement park development in the north-eastern United States, and Geoffrey Thompson took the opportunity to observe, compare and develop contacts. We see this process at work in a letter from his father to Brady McSwiggan of Kennywood in 1960, while he was enjoying his time at business school: 'The letters we receive from him indicate that he is having the whale of a time, though I trust, from the money it is costing, that he is also doing some hard work in his spare time...' Leonard Thompson went on to suggest that the McSwiggans invite Geoffrey over for 'the odd square meal', while adding a jocular warning not to 'lend him any money on my account. I understand that these days American girls are very expensive.' The same letter also showed that the Thompsons continued in friendly contact with Ray Lusse, who was still involved in the shared Blackpool amusement machinery enterprise, and it was into this informal freemasonry of amusement park businesses that Geoffrey Thompson was being inducted.[45]

Like his father, Geoffrey Thompson had the opportunity to serve a short apprenticeship in business away from the Pleasure Beach, working in London for New Era Laundries during an expansionist phase of the company's activities. He was brought home in 1963 when the manager of the

[44] Bennett, *Century of Fun*, pp. 102–4; http://www.etext.virginia.edu/railton/tomsawye/nostalgiadisneyhmp.html accessed 19 Aug. 2006.

[45] Martin Wainwright, obituary of Geoffrey Thompson, *Guardian*, 30 June 2004; http://www.themagiceye.co.uk/d158.html Leonard Thompson to Brady McSwiggan, 16 Mar. 1960, accessed 19 Aug. 2006; Pleasure Beach Archive, Cuttings Books, *World's Fair*, 11 May 1957.

Casino departed unexpectedly, and took over the management of the catering and entertainment there. By the time his father died he had spent thirteen years working for the company, mainly looking after the Pleasure Beach's interests at the neighbouring Lancashire seaside amusement parks at Southport and Morecambe, which were viewed as complementary with rather than competitors of the Pleasure Beach. Leonard Thompson had kept a very tight hold on the day-to-day running of the Pleasure Beach itself, while living at his rural retreat on the edge of the Bowland fells and presenting an increasingly austere face to the world. A *Daily Express* feature of 1966 emphasized his formal demeanour and self-contained isolation, with the calm of his secluded office amid the Pleasure Beach hubbub 'like entering a cathedral from an Italian street', and passed on his view that 'most of Blackpool is ugly', especially the Golden Mile sea-front. Two years earlier the same newspaper had claimed that, because of his university education and air of academic detachment, he was widely known on the Pleasure Beach as 'the Prof'.[46] An enduring concern for the order and respectability that Leonard Thompson prized was underlined by the Pleasure Beach's refusal to allow local pop group The Reverend Black and the Rocking Vicars to appear at the Casino in the late 1960s, because the band's 'name and general presentation', featuring a lipstick-smeared gilded crucifix, was 'not in keeping with family entertainment'; but Screaming Lord Sutch was acceptable soon afterwards, with a support act called 'Stoned Rose' and the promise of 'Booze till Midnite'.[47] Geoffrey Thompson was quite at home with this, as the mid-1960s saw the opening of a sequence of themed bars at the Casino, as part of his father's development plan but under his immediate management. The Gaslight Bar of 1964 had an Edwardian theme, aiming to 'capture the full flavour of the good old days', and featuring a polyphon that Geoffrey Thompson had found in a local second-hand shop, together with gas light fittings and furniture acquired from old pubs. This commercial interest in nostalgia, which in this case anticipated later trends by at least a decade, was to be a theme of Geoffrey Thompson's stewardship of the Pleasure Beach, and it seems to have paid. The bar soon became 'crammed with young men with very white shirts and signet rings who look like (the fashionable actor) Albert Finney, and their nubile young women.' At the same time Diamond Lil's 'saloon' provided a Wild West theme with can-can dancers and a very lively atmosphere. The Paradise Room, which opened a year later, offered continental sophistication of a kind more in keeping with Leonard Thompson's preferences, together with

46 Pleasure Beach Archive, Cuttings Books, 1953–69, *Daily Express*, 12 May 1964, 1 July 1966.

47 Ibid., *Daily Telegraph*, no date; 1969–74, press advertisement, no date.

the late opening hours that accompanied this image; but Geoffrey Thompson's management of the Casino during the 1960s gave strong hints of a new regime in the making alongside the old, more than a decade before his father's death. Taking over responsibility for the whole enormous enterprise, however, was an altogether more demanding matter.[48]

The successor regime had to hit the ground running. One of his sisters had 'chosen not to be directly involved' in the business, and the other had been killed in an air crash; so Geoffrey Thompson was the only available member of the family to carry on the succession. He was also able and willing to take on the task, and proved more than equal to it. Under his regime the Pleasure Beach sustained an accelerating rhythm of innovation and diversification, reaching out to new markets, becoming genuinely international in its influence, and achieving spectacular publicity for its new rides, on a scale that went beyond the promotional and publicity successes of the 1930s. These further dimensions to the Pleasure Beach's image and prosperity were developed under the chairmanship of Leonard Thompson's widow, Doris, who was a highly astute and experienced figure in local Conservative politics and in voluntary organisations, and whose willingness to try out new rides and act out an important ceremonial role into her nineties was supplemented by what was obviously a keen business brain. Geoffrey Thompson became managing director, and his wife Barbara, the daughter of a local solicitor, also joined the board. The family business had successfully made the notoriously difficult transition from the second generation to the third, aided by a powerful continuing presence from the founder's daughter.[49]

Just as his father had done in the 1930s, Geoffrey Thompson brought a new impetus and an awareness of current trends in tourism and entertainment to the Pleasure Beach. He was an ebullient character, memorably described by the novelist Andrew Martin as 'half circus ringmaster, half Cambridge-educated economist'.[50] After an initial homage to the wishes of his father, who had been planning to add scenes from the Angkor Wat temples to the River Caves after a visit to Cambodia towards the end of his life, the new regime focused on holding prices steady in an inflationary period while investing in spectacular new rides and promoting them with imaginative attention to publicity. This policy began with the Steeplechase, which was designed by Arrow Engineering and installed by the Pleasure Beach staff, and featured individual racehorses running on parallel tracks

48 Ibid., 1953–69, *West Lancashire Evening Gazette*, 24 Mar. 1964, 5 May 1964, 6 July 1965.
49 Bennett, *Century of Fun*, pp. 105–7.
50 Andrew Martin, 'The Rollercoaster Champion of the World', *Granta* 79, http://www.granta.com/extracts/1855 accessed 30 Sept. 2006.

over a course that covered nearly half a mile. Its cost of £813,000 made it comfortably the most expensive Pleasure Beach installation to date, and its inauguration featured the legendary steeplechaser and Grand National winner Red Rum and a display by the Red Arrows formation flying team, fuelling a blaze of publicity.[51]

Nearly thirty years later, the Steeplechase was capable of attracting a sympathetic if not uncritical review from a roller coaster enthusiast, who set it in the context of Geoffrey Thompson's own sympathetic understanding of the history of the business in which he had grown up. The Pleasure Beach was 'famous for its collection of old-fashioned and unusual rides... The Steeplechase is a shining example of a ride that screamed the word "strange".' It harked back consciously to the earliest rides at Coney Island's Steeplechase Park, and it was praiseworthy as a custom-built ride rather than something taken 'off the peg' at a difficult time in the industry, although its long queues, based on inadequate information and low throughput rather than overwhelming popularity, together with the roughness of the ride and an anticlimactic last section, denied it a high star rating. It was, however, a vote of confidence in the Pleasure Beach's future at a time of intensifying competition in the holiday and entertainment industries, and in many ways its self-confidence, sheer ambition, and the panache of its launching ceremony made it the shape of things to come for the next quarter of a century and beyond.[52]

The year 1977 was transitional in other ways. The introduction of a Go-Kart track and an 'antique Carousel' acquired from Porthcawl provided further early illustrations of Geoffrey Thompson's characteristic combination of alertness to current trends and awareness of the commercial value of a sense of fairground history, but the reconstruction of Emberton's Casino was an important symbolic recognition of the need for renewal under the new management. Geoffrey Thompson spent one and three-quarter million pounds on a complete makeover for the building, which was beginning to show evidence of wear and tear and needed internal rearrangement to meet changing tastes and expectations. Keith Ingham of Preston's Building Design Partnership oversaw the conversion, and (as with previous Pleasure Beach appointments) there was nothing parochial or conservative about the choice of architect. Ingham may have been the son of a builder from nearby St Annes, but he had trained at the Bartlett School, was responsible for the enormous Preston Bus Station of the late 1960s, was one of the

51 Bennett, *Century of Fun*, pp. 107–9.

52 http://www.s104638357.websitehome.co.uk/html/steeplechase_main.htm accessed 21 Aug. 2006.

founders of what became the Urban Design Group in 1978, and had served as vice-president of the Royal Institute of British Architects in 1968-9. He was a major figure in post-war modernist architecture in Britain; and he also went on record as expressing scepticism about the corporate and uniform nature of the architecture of the redeveloped Golden Mile, complaining that its character (and some of its popularity) had been lost through a drive to uniformity and impersonality, which were clearly outcomes to be avoided on the Pleasure Beach.[53] New bars and restaurants were introduced, together with a new top floor which included the Calypso Bar; a Hollywood nostalgia 'dark ride' on the first floor, designed by Maurice Ayers, who had previously been responsible for the Gold Mine; an external elevator in the form of a glass pod, the first such installation in Britain; and a monorail extension around the curve of the first floor, complete with its own station.[54]

The new management regime also made an immediate difference to Pleasure Beach interests at Southport and Morecambe. Geoffrey Thompson began a major development programme at Morecambe, even as the resort as a whole fell into accelerating decline,[55] and invested nearly six million pounds in the Pleasure Park over the next decade. At Southport he completed the acquisition of Helters and Hotchkiss, which operated important rides and in both of which the Pleasure Beach had been the dominant influence, in 1977, and five years later took out a 60-year lease on Pleasureland from the local authority which owned and ran the park. This completed a process which had begun before the Second World War and had failed to come to fruition in the immediate post-war years, when Leonard Thompson had been on the verge of reaching an agreement with Southport Corporation. Local government reorganisation in 1974 found the new Sefton council more amenable to a private enterprise takeover than Southport had been. This gave the Pleasure Beach an overarching set of complementary interests along the Lancashire holiday coast on either side of Blackpool itself.[56]

Meanwhile, just as the growth of the popular overseas package holiday market went into overdrive, the late 1970s and early 1980s saw a continued spurt of investment in new attractions, while control of the Morecambe and Southport amusement parks enabled the less iconic rides to be rotated

53 http://groups.msn.com/TheSavePrestonBusStationCampaign/heritagenote3.msnw accessed 16 Sept. 2006; *West Lancashire Evening Gazette*, 20 July 1977.

54 Bennett, *Century of Fun*, pp. 109–10.

55 R. Bingham, *Lost Resort? The Flow and Ebb of Morecambe* (Milnthorpe, 1991).

56 Bennett, *Century of Fun*, pp. 112–13; Copnall, *Pleasureland Memories*, pp. 44–50, 72–3.

**The Revolution, Britain's first steel looping coaster, was to date relatively quickly, but its introduction coincided with a major intensification of competition in international tourism markets and it provided strong publicity and new excitement at a time when these were particularly necessary. The 'busy' nature of the Pleasure Beach, with its tightly-packed intersecting rides offering interesting views of each other as they crossed and re-crossed, is evident here.**

between the sites. In 1979 Arrow provided the Revolution, the first million-pound ride on the Pleasure Beach. It followed three years behind the inauguration of the first Revolution at Magic Mountain, in the United States, in 1976, but was not quite the first steel looping coaster in Europe, as the German firm Schwarzkopf had put the Looping Star out on the German fairground circuit in 1978. It dated quickly as loops and inversions spread rapidly through the inland theme parks that were proliferating in Britain during the 1980s, but at the time it provided an exciting new accent on the Pleasure Beach skyline when viewed from the promenade, and it still receives praise from reviewers for its compactness and the thrill of the first drop.[57] At the same time a Water Chute arrived, in belated replacement of the ride that had been lost in 1933; but this was less of a novelty, having been

57 http://www.s104638357.websitehome.co.uk/html/revolution_main.htm accessed 30 Sept. 2006.

originally installed at Manchester's Belle Vue in 1957. In 1980, a further million pounds paid for the installation of several smaller new rides. This phase of heavy investment produced the Tidal Wave (a pirate ship ride), the Swamp Buggies ('a Dodgem track on water'), the Haunted Hotel, the Tokaydo Express (a figure-of-eight steel roller-coaster aimed at a family market), and other less lasting installations, some of which had moved on within a few years. One nostalgic observer remarked on the plethora of 'portable rides that flooded the South Park in the eighties', off-the-peg and often readily portable touring fairground attractions from established firms like Huss; and this groundswell of shifting variety provided the backdrop to the regular introduction of the star rides. None were as ephemeral as the skateboard park of 1978, which failed to anticipate the long-term popularity of the craze and closed almost as soon as it opened.[58]

After this dramatic, and in part experimental, expansion of the range of rides on offer, and the diversification into additional amusement sites on the Lancashire coast, the Pleasure Beach began to develop its international dimensions. In 1982 it made an ultimately ill-starred attempt at expansion into the United States, as Geoffrey Thompson paid a million dollars to take over the site of the accident-prone and by this time defunct Wild, Wild West theme park at Magic Harbor, South Carolina, and established the British Amusement Park, with promotional material that proclaimed, 'It's Great Rides. It's Live Entertainment. It's Great British Fun,' with prominent displays of the union flag and supporting copy that began, 'What's red, white and blue all over? It's Magic Harbor, Myrtle Beach's own British Amusement Park.' There were more than twenty rides in a woodland setting with a scattering of lakes, in a landscape far removed from Blackpool's South Shore in every respect, although the live shows included 'Startime on Ice', produced by Geoffrey Thompson's daughter Amanda, as well as Country Connection and Wonderland of Magic. There was a 150-foot Ferris Wheel, brought across the Atlantic from Morecambe after opposition from the local authority there, and a steel coaster called the Black Witch, as well as the King Charles English Pub where 'mom and dad can relax while the kids enjoy the park'. The uncertain tone of the advertising material, not quite in tune with a transatlantic public, probably helps to explain why the idea did not work, even in one of the fastest-growing American cities of the late twentieth century; and the experiment was faltering financially when a fatality on the Black Witch helped to sign its death warrant and, in 1992, the Pleasure Beach abandoned Magic Harbor. This attempted reversal of

[58] Bennett, *Century of Fun*, pp. 115–17; http://www.themagiceye.co.uk/lostrides.html accessed 30 Sept. 2006.

**Eddie 'The Eagle' Edwards was, from a publicity point of view, one of the Pleasure Beach's better choices for the launch of a new ride, the Avalanche of 1988: he was both a classic underdog in his sporting field and an assertive defender of his right to compete in the Winter Olympics, and he was a popular figure on both counts.**

the original transatlantic relationship, in which the credibility had flowed eastwards across the Atlantic from Coney Island and the American amusement industry to Blackpool, along with most of the technology, was even less effective in outcomes than in presentation, although the ambitious attempt did reflect the changing balance of dynamism and success in the contrast between the long-term decline of the American amusement park industry and the contrasting buoyancy of the Pleasure Beach.[59]

This was not the only international venture. The Ice Drome, with a much reduced cast but increasingly dramatic special effects for 'Showtime on Ice' from 1978 onwards, began to export its shows not only within Britain and Ireland, but also, in 1978-9, to the Middle East, although a successful visit to the United Arab Emirates and another to Tehran, unfortunately coinciding with the revolution against the Shah, were not followed up. In 1980 Robin Cousins, the ice-dancing gold medallist at the Winter Olympics, began an association with the Pleasure Beach, and three years later Gloria Gee was moved from producing cabaret at the Horseshoe Bar to running the ice shows, recruiting a genuinely international cast from

59 Bennett, *Century of Fun*, pp. 113–14; Bennett, *Hot Ice*, pp. 60–1; Jones and Wills, *Invention of the Park*, p. 113; Bret Malone, 'Magic Harbor', http://www.defunctparks.com accessed 20 March 2006.

(among other places) the United States, South Korea and South Africa. New lighting systems, a new production team and a new title, 'The Hot Ice Show', refreshed the format.[60] A genuinely global development was the Blackpool Leisure and Amusement Consultancy, established in 1982 to give a focused commercial identity to the export of Pleasure Beach expertise that had already been a regular feature of the 1930s. The highest profile amusement park in which the Pleasure Beach was involved, originally envisaged as Nehruland but relabelled as Esselworld by the time of its opening, was developed from 1988 on an island near Mumbai (then still known as Bombay) and close to Bollywood, under the auspices of the grain export, storage, packaging and later media tycoon Subhash Chandra.[61]

But the Pleasure Beach remained essentially a British concern, and its future did not lie in multiplying new ventures across cultures and continents. The Blackpool operation remained central to the whole enterprise, although in 1987 Geoffrey Thompson inaugurated a transformation of the Morecambe Pleasure Park, which was re-themed under the management of his architect daughter Fiona. It became Frontierland, celebrating the American Wild West, and this helped annual visitor numbers to grow tenfold in twenty years, from a mere 80,000 in 1970 to 800,000 in 1990. It was an outpost of growth in an increasingly desolate setting, as Morecambe's overall holiday economy went into free fall.[62] At the Blackpool site, another million-pound ride, the Space Invader, was inaugurated in 1984. This dark ride from the German manufacturer Zierer, which started 72 feet up inside a 'mountain' and simulated a space voyage, cashed in on the current vogue for primitive 'space invaders' electronic games in pubs and arcades. It used the current 'Dr Who' to perform the opening ceremony, and was backed up by an aggressive television advertising campaign which built up the ride as the ultimate in thrills. The Pleasure Beach management was by this time well practised in making the most of the publicity opportunities that surrounded a striking new ride, and similar campaigns were to punctuate the next two decades, at regular intervals.[63] Four years later a further spectacular new ride, the Avalanche, made an even greater impact. It was one of three new bobsleigh coasters to be installed by another German firm, Heinrich Mack, in 1988, the other two being in Mack's own showcase Europa Park

[60] Bennett, *Hot Ice*, pp. 51–61.

[61] Bennett, *Century of Fun*, p. 114; http://www.esselworld.com accessed 30 Sept. 2006.

[62] Bennett, *Century of Fun*, p. 113; J. Urry, 'Lancaster: small firms, tourism and the "locality"', in M. Harloe, C.G. Pickvance and J. Urry (eds.), *Place, Policy and Politics* (London, 1990), pp. 161–2.

[63] http://www.s104638357.websitehome.co.uk/html/spaceinvader2_main.htm accessed 30 Sept. 2006; http://www.themagiceye.co.uk/space2.html accessed 30 Sept. 2006.

**The building of Ocean Boulevard marked a more assertive attitude to the Pleasure Beach's presentation of itself to the outside world, taking the opportunity that eventually became available to capitalise on the retailing potential of the South Promenade, on which it had previously been required to turn its back.**

in Germany, and in Richmond, Virginia. Publicity was guaranteed by the Pleasure Beach's sponsorship of the British bobsleigh team in a Winter Olympics year, by the ride's record cost of £2.5 million, and by an appropriate choice of celebrity for the opening ceremony, the British ski-jumper Eddie 'The Eagle' Edwards, the perfect emblem of gallant sporting failure. He was certainly an improvement on the choice of Lord Thorneycroft, the then Chairman of the Conservative Party and an unexciting figure, a former Chancellor of the Exchequer and keen supporter of Margaret Thatcher with a low profile outside the ranks of the Party faithful, to share the opening of the new Water Chute nine years earlier. This had been a rare example of party political ties coming before commercial publicity needs, and over the ensuing decade the Pleasure Beach had adapted very quickly and with increasing sophistication to changing media perceptions and expectations. The impact of the Avalanche and its associated publicity was measurable in the Pleasure Beach's takings: its turnover increased by 27 per cent to £22 million between 1987 and 1988, and attendances reached the

6.5 million per year around which they were to fluctuate into the new millennium. This was a triumphant investment.[64]

The Pleasure Beach management took this opportunity, in 1989, to update basic amenities and enhance the retail side of the business, which was becoming increasingly important to all branches of the theme park, museum and heritage sectors. Piecemeal improvements to existing catering outlets were not enough. A Blackpool architect, Gordon MacKeith, whose family firm had been established in the town since 1926 and had done restoration work on Frank Matcham's Grand Theatre, was engaged to oversee a range of projects. A new Superloo complex brought necessary reassurance about cleanliness and comfort to families who might have worried about accusations of tackiness and dirt. The choice of Sir Cyril Smith, the very large Liberal MP for Rochdale, to perform the opening ceremony reinforced ties with the traditional visitor hinterland and the culture of the comic postcard, while implicitly drawing attention to the solidity and stability of the equipment. Other aspects of the refurbishment reinforced management's commitment to the recognition and celebration of Pleasure Beach history and heritage, as in the 1930s Art Deco style adopted for the Casino's revamped Beach Restaurant, the opening of a Museum of the Pleasure Beach, and the introduction of a new retail unit underneath the Sir Hiram Maxim ride which underlined its historic importance to the park. These and other projects accounted for £2.5 million, and a further £9 million was committed to the development of a shopping and restaurant complex facing the Promenade, where the original agreement with the Corporation had required a blank façade. Ocean Boulevard, as it was named, had an Edwardian architectural theme reminiscent of the Spanish Street and similar themed arrangements of shops and booths within the Pleasure Beach before the First World War, and it also included 'oriental' touches that echoed the original Casino. But the name itself looked across the Atlantic to Myrtle Beach, where Geoffrey Thompson's British theme park was still operating, although the cultural referents included a joke shop named for the English comedian Tommy Cooper as well as the only British branch of Ripley's Odditorium, a 'Fisherman's Wharf' in minor homage to San Francisco, and a classic American diner. As with so much of the historic Pleasure Beach, Ocean Boulevard was an Anglo-American hybrid in which a great deal of specifically British popular culture was firmly embedded.[65]

[64] Bennett, *Century of Fun*, pp. 115, 119; www.themagiceye.co.uk/avalanche.html accessed 30 Sept. 2006.

[65] Bennett, *Century of Fun*, pp. 121–3.

In the aftermath of this diversification the profile of the business had changed considerably. By 1993 the rides themselves generated just 55 per cent of the Pleasure Beach's business, while the catering outlets produced 25 per cent and the retail units 8 per cent. But the Pleasure Beach's dominant identity for publicity and image purposes was that of 'Rollercoaster Capital of the World', and this in turn underlined the continuing importance of its own history and heritage. At the beginning of the 1990s Emberton's station for the Grand National, which was showing its age, was carefully rebuilt in its original style under MacKeith's supervision, and a carousel imported from Mangels of Coney Island in 1919 was restored by Jacksons of Congleton, a specialist fairground ride manufacturer which would be known to Pleasure Beach management through its concession at Southport's Pleasureland. There was also some adaptation of existing rides, as when the Autoskooters of 1929 were redesigned by Thompson's daughter Fiona, now Fiona Gilje, with an American Superbowl theme. In 1993 the National Amusement Park Historical Association of the United States made Geoffrey Thompson its first life member and gave him a special award for his work in maintaining and conserving historic rides, which acquired commemorative plaques in an American style to explain their historical significance.[66]

But all this activity coincided with a damaging loss. Fire was a recurrent hazard at the Pleasure Beach, though not to the same extent as the Coney Island parks, where the construction materials used had been flimsier and more inflammable. Blazes were normally contained without extensive damage, though the destruction of the Indian Pavilion shortly before the Second World War had been a costly exception. But the fire in the Fun House in December 1991 was a very serious matter, destroying an iconic building and a large amount of equipment that was in storage, including items of historic significance. The Laughing Man figure was also destroyed, although his head had been removed for repair work; and the total damage was estimated at £10 million. This was a severe commercial blow, and left a gaping hole not only in the amusement park's range of attractions, but also in the mental maps and memories of those who had enjoyed the Fun House in the past.[67]

The Pleasure Beach was trying to consolidate for further growth in an increasingly competitive environment, as new theme parks proliferated

66 Ibid., pp. 124–5, 132; http://nfa.dept.shef.ac.uk/history/rides/super_bob.php accessed 1 Oct. 2006.

67 Bennett, *Century of Fun*, pp. 125–6.

away from the coast from the 1980s, not all of them successfully, while a whole new market in heritage tourism opened out, especially on old industrial sites and in former industrial towns.[68] EuroDisney also seemed likely to be a competitive threat, but reassurances from Disney planners on their visit to the Pleasure Beach in 1991 turned out to be well founded: Disney was not competing for the same markets, though they might overlap, and its presence in northern France raised the profile of other European theme and amusement parks on an international stage. The Pleasure Beach responded by increasing the volume and profile of its advertising, co-operating with the local authority and with First Leisure, the other dominant Blackpool entertainment corporation; and 1993 proved to be another excellent season after an interlude of uncertainty, with visitor numbers up to 6.7 million and turnover up by 13 per cent on the previous year. This was the prelude to the introduction of the most spectacular new ride of all in the following year.[69]

The Pepsi Max Big One was, for two years, the world's tallest, fastest and steepest roller coaster; and more than a decade after its opening it was still the tallest ride in Britain. It was a triumph of engineering and of the imaginative and economical use of space on a cramped and crowded site; but above all, it was a triumph of publicity and the manipulation of symbolism. The construction of this high profile attraction, which towered 235 feet above the promenade at its highest point and boasted a passenger capacity of 1,700 per hour, was trailed for two years beforehand. The excitement was fuelled by an accelerating rhythm of media speculation and progress reports as the foundations were prepared during 1992–3 and the superstructure set up, against the clock, during the winter and spring of 1993–4. The combination of a trusted American ride design and engineering firm, Arrow Dynamics, and an in-house architect, Geoffrey Thompson's daughter Fiona Gilje, followed well-established Pleasure Beach practice, and the design of the station was an economical use of space and verticality on a site where every inch was precious, just as the coaster route itself was fitted in with minimum disruption to the established layout and maximum visual interaction with existing rides, not to mention exciting panoramas across the Irish Sea and the roofs of Blackpool for those who were prepared to look at them. The cost of the installation, whether it was £12 or 13 million, was arresting in its own right; and the media attention given to this crowning glory of the Pleasure Beach, and challenging new accent on the Blackpool

68 Cross and Walton, *Playful Crowd*, Chapter 6; Robert Hewison, *The Heritage Industry* (London, 1987).

69 Bennett, *Century of Fun*, p. 129.

**The construction of the Big One during 1993–4 was a visitor attraction in its own right, and provided regular publicity opportunities in the run-up to the opening of the Pleasure Beach's single most successful investment, which outshone the Tower centenary in 1994 and planted a conspicuous new accent on Blackpool's skyline, which was easily visible from the Bowland fells more than thirty miles from the resort itself.**

skyline, hijacked a large proportion of the publicity the town reaped from the centenary of the opening of Blackpool Tower and of the Grand Theatre, casting a shadow over the equally impressive investment by First Leisure in an extensive makeover of the Tower itself. The ride itself proved commercially successful, although the opening ceremony was eventually entrusted to Bad Boys Inc, a boy band whose career proved to be as ephemeral as it was meteoric, spanning a mere two years, five hits and a single album, and a minor collision soon after the opening generated a burst of adverse publicity. Many coaster enthusiasts regarded the ride as disappointing, after the early thrill of the first big drop: there was little of the 'air time' that they prized, and one perceptive commentator remarked that the experience was, in effect, more visual than visceral, with normal trains and an absence of gimmicks or inversions. This was a straightforward, old-fashioned coaster ride on the grand scale, communicating an expectation of terror by its sheer size, and giving most of its customers the satisfaction of having accomplished a frightening mission. In fact, older rides like the Grand National and Wild Mouse were much more exciting and challenging, and 'this combination of the traditional and the modern is the hallmark of the Pleasure Beach.'[70]

The Big One was a tremendous success. David Cam, a long-serving Pleasure Beach director, told the Blackpool hearing of the national casino enquiry in 2006 that it 'generated an increase in 35% of the visitors to Blackpool Pleasure Beach which... is 1.8 million people in one year, to see that attraction, if not to ride it.' It took its place alongside the Tower in the redefinition of the popular place-myth of Blackpool, and gave the Pleasure Beach a special place on the amusement park map of Britain and beyond. It marked the climax of Geoffrey Thompson's stewardship of the Pleasure Beach. He continued with the policy of introducing an eye-catching new ride every two years or so, and a bigger and more expensive novelty at slightly longer intervals: the Valhalla dark water ride, at a cost of £15 million, in 2000, with the Ice Blast ride and its 210-foot tower filling the gap in 1997 and the Spin Doctor and Bling following on in 2002 and 2004. Reviews of Valhalla run across the spectrum from dismissive to euphoric, bringing out the problems as well as the glories of the Pleasure Beach at the turn of the millennium. Enthusiasts for the ride praise the excitement, the unpredictability of the darkness, and the contrasts between fire and ice; critics complain about the sheer volume of water and, more damagingly, the tackiness and unreliability of some of the special effects as well as the lack of a clear story line and the absence of animatronics. As some of the reviewers point out, the Pleasure Beach is not Disney, and its policy is to prioritise special effects over fantasy narratives; but the comments about visible cost cutting and lack of maintenance, coupled with scepticism about the real level of investment, are potentially damaging to the credibility of the enterprise, although there are also 'post-tourists' among the reviewers who enjoy the occasionally ramshackle aspects of the Pleasure Beach, regarding them as an essential part of the experience.[71]

70 Ibid., pp. 133–9; http://www.s104638357.websitehome.co.uk/html/birthday_bigoneconst.htm and http://www.s104638357.websitehome.co.uk/html/birthday_bigten.htm accessed 7 Oct. 2006; J.M. Roberts, 'The "Pepsi Max Big One" Rollercoaster – Blackpool Pleasure Beach', *Structural Engineer* 72 (21), 1 Nov. 1994; http://www.culture.gov.uk/Cap/eip/eip_docs/blackpool/Blackpool_transcript.pdf p. 46, evidence of David Cam, accessed 19 May 2007.

71 Evidence of David Cam, cited above, note 70, pp. 26, 76; http://www.themeparkinsider.com/reviews/blackpool_pleasure_beach accessed 7 Oct. 2006; http://www.s104638357.websitehome.co.uk/html/valhalla_yourthoughts.htm accessed 7 Oct. 2006.

The Pleasure Beach under Geoffrey Thompson has been described as 'a working museum of the amusement park industry'.[72] For many visitors at, and before, the turn of the millennium, its special qualities lay in the sheer variety of rides, of different ages and contrasting specifications, operating cheek by jowl on a cramped and crowded site. This is a far cry from the modernist vision of organized chaos and ordered disorder that was propagated by Leonard Thompson and Joseph Emberton in their bid to construct a clean, streamlined, respectable amusement park in the 1930s. This project lost its way during the post-war hiatus when no further development could be undertaken, and when the Festival of Britain styles of the 1950s failed to capture the popular imagination as 1930s modernism had sometimes been capable of doing. Under Geoffrey Thompson, especially, the Pleasure Beach reverted to being a conglomeration of rides, interspersed more thoroughly with food and retail outlets, some of them increasingly themed and sophisticated, but without any overall sense of plan or order. From being conceived as an ordered whole, the park reverted to an anarchic (and often enjoyable) jumble, with random and shifting highlights and (after the sponsorship of the Big One) an increasing concern for generating sponsorship revenues and associated labelling which grated on some of the older enthusiasts. Geoffrey Thompson's enthusiasm for the park's history, and his urge to replicate and commemorate the past, coexisted with the loss of the wider vision whose component parts he was so anxious to conserve or celebrate. His premature death in 2004, closely followed by that of his mother, brought the Pleasure Beach to another moment of transition, as the succession passed to his daughter Amanda, who had been more concerned with the development of the shows than with the working of the amusement parks.

The transfer of power came at a difficult point, and it soon became apparent that the Pleasure Beach was entering another transitional phase in its history. When the Casino Advisory Panel came to Blackpool in September 2006 to hear the town's case to house the first new super-casino in Britain, David Cam's evidence painted a gloomy picture. Visitor numbers had been declining since 1997, had fallen by 7 per cent in 2005 and were projected to suffer a similar decline in 2006, as the Pleasure Beach considered making over 20 per cent of its 'loyal and long-serving' labour force redundant. The company aimed to try to spend its way out of recession in time-honoured style, by introducing a startling new multi-million pound

72 http://www.s104638357.websitehome.co.uk/html/revolution_main.htm accessed 30 Sept. 2006.

attraction in 2007; but management was uncertain about what would follow.[73] In 2006 it employed around 2000 full- and part-time staff and brought in £70 million per year to the local economy, but was not recognised as an industry for the purposes of attracting any kind of business grant aid, while almost all of the region's tourism development grant aid went to Greater Manchester (especially) and Merseyside.[74] The sudden closure of Pleasureland at Southport at the end of the 2006 season,[75] following that of Frontierland in 2000, together with the confirmation under the new regime of Geoffrey Thompson's decision to abandon historic and established rides such as the Turtle Chase and the Whip at Blackpool and followed by the dismantling of the Log Flume, communicated an air of uncertainty about the immediate future of the Geoffrey Thompson legacy. In 2005 the Coaster Kingdom website mourned the loss of the Turtle Chase and Whip thus: 'Touching either the historical Whip or Turtle Chase verges on blasphemy at the cathedral of historic amusement rides, Blackpool, yet in a quite remarkable move, both Whip and Turtle Chase are being removed from Pleasure Beach Blackpool's 2005 line-up.' The loss of existing rides, on Blackpool's cramped and crowded site, was a necessary price to pay to make room for the new, but the Pleasure Beach's 'rich heritage is normally spared.'[76] In the autumn of 2006 the Pleasure Beach showed its awareness of the marketability of memories of and attachments to its discarded rides by offering the ride cars from the Turtle Chase for sale on the internet, urging visitors to the park's own website to 'buy your own piece of history on Ebay now.'[77]

Meanwhile members of the Pleasure Beach 235 Club were sharing the excitement of anticipating a major new ride, promised for the 2007 season, even as they were offered a special event to commemorate the last rites on

[73] http://www.blackpooltoday.co.uk/ViewArticle2 accessed 16 Sept. 2006; http://www.culture.gov.uk/Cap/eip/eip_docs/blackpool/Blackpool_transcript.pdf evidence of David Cam, p. 45, accessed 19 May 2007.

[74] ODPM, 2006, Blackpool Council, p. 149.

[75] Southport's MP John Pugh associated the closure with the change of regime after Geoffrey Thompson's death, commenting that 'recent charging regimes for admission looked suicidal and seem to have backfired horribly', while marketing was 'underplayed'. He wondered whether the Pleasure Beach was retrenching against the possibility of Blackpool failing to secure the proposed super-casino: http://www.johnpughmp.com/pressrelease.htm 4 Sept. 2006, accessed 4 Nov. 2006.

[76] http://www.S104638357.websitehome.co.uk/html/magazine_03_-01.htm accessed 28 Oct. 2006.

[77] http://www.blackpoolpleasurebeach.com accessed 28 Oct. 2006; thanks to Jason Wood for alerting me to this.

the Log Flume, and as makeovers were announced for Noah's Ark and the Grand National.[78] The new ride, Infusion, billed as the world's first suspended looping rollercoaster completely over water, officially cost £8 million as against the £18-20 million that the Pleasure Beach had hoped to raise for a more spectacular installation projecting over the sea. It was really the Traumatizer from the abandoned Pleasureland at Southport, relocated and with an enhanced image. Pleasure Beach publicity made much of the exciting dictionary meanings of 'infusion', but the dominant, and confusing, images were of herbal tea and of a Blackpool swingers' club which had anticipated the name. A commentator on the 'Coaster Kingdom' website thought the ride looked exciting with the added water, but had serious reservations about the new management: 'Amanda Thompson has become the wicked witch of the west coast due to removing more rides, often of historical merit, while adding very little.' He hoped that it would pave the way for more exciting investment in the near future, but his expectations were not high.[79] The auguries were confusing, and the future relationship between profit, novelty, heritage and nostalgia under the new management regime remains unclear. The Pleasure Beach's strong support for Blackpool's bid for a regional casino in 2006 showed awareness of a need for regeneration across the resort as a whole, and the unsatisfactory failure of central government to resolve this issue was very frustrating for the management. But it is too soon to develop a convincing historical perspective on these current events. We shall have to wait and see.

78 http://www.235club.co.uk/news/news_06.22.html accessed 28 Oct. 2006.

79 http://www.a2mediagroup.com/?c=1248&a=14882 accessed 19 May 2007; http://www.s104638357.websitehome.co.uk/html/2006/11/infusion.html accessed 19 May 2007; http://www.culture.gov.uk/Cap/eip/eip_docs/blackpool/Blackpool_transcript.pdf, evidence of David Cam, p. 76, accessed 19 May 2007.

# 5 Customers and Workers

**An odd mixture of people posing for the camera in 1907, including manual workers, men in naval style uniform or fragments of it, and two 'respectable' looking teenagers, one female. This looks more like the celebration of a finished project than a group of holidaymakers.**

After charting the changing fortunes of the Pleasure Beach and its relationship with Blackpool over the turbulent twentieth century, we now focus more directly on the customers and workforce who made the whole story possible. The customers created the atmosphere and animation of the crowd at play, while their spending on rides, stalls, shows, souvenirs and fast food kept this commercial enterprise in being, pushed it into endless innovation and adaptation, and sustained its unique reputation within Blackpool and in the world at large. The workforce, many of them seasonal, insecure and lacking in officially recognised skills, but in many cases adaptable, hard-working over long hours, and capable of picking up the necessary know-how on the job, and sometimes being promoted within the enterprise, were essential to the Pleasure Beach's success and to the creation of its distinctive identity. This chapter looks at these overlapping groups of

A packed but characteristically orderly Pleasure Beach crowd of the 1920s. The scene features older attractions like the Rainbow Wheel, the Helter Skelter, the Scenic Railway and the Monitor and Merrimac auditorium. Young people are in short supply, and hats are still de rigueur, although the humble flat cap is much in evidence. A few early nonconformists of both sexes go bare-headed in the bottom left-hand corner.

people (customers might also be or become workers, and the other way round) and at the relationships between them.

We lack the kind of evidence that might let us count and analyse the Pleasure Beach's visitors in conventional ways: where they came from, what their jobs were, how old they were, whether they came as individuals, couples, families or groups of friends and workmates. Until the last few years there have been no censuses of Pleasure Beach visitors, and those that have been undertaken remain, understandably, commercially confidential. David Cam told the national Casino enquiry in 2006 that '90% of our visitors are from social categories C and D', or routine clerical and manual workers with limited scope for increased spending power; and he also emphasised the Pleasure Beach's focus on families. Material from Pleasure Beach surveys also tells us that in 2004 Pleasure Beach visitors were more likely to stay overnight in Blackpool (56 per cent against 44) than the general run of Blackpool visitors (54:46), while the peak period for Pleasure Beach customers at this time was still August, followed by September, although the percentage figures supplied to Blackpool Council for the Casino bid add up to 98.5 rather than a hundred.[1] But to find out more about the visitors, we have to take a different route, looking at visual evidence from photographs, films and cartoons, and at what others said about the Pleasure Beach and its people.

Most of the commentary on the customers and their behaviour has come from outsiders, from people who formed part of the crowd temporarily and observed or took part in its amusements in order to write about it for other people's consumption, rather than going with family, friends, workmates and neighbours to enjoy the Pleasure Beach as an exciting experience in its own right. The further back we go in time, the more the sources are dominated by journalists and writers of travel guides and social commentary, usually with an agenda of their own, rather than by ordinary customers describing the pleasures they derive from their visits. We also have visual evidence, especially in the form of photographs, but here again we are at the mercy of the angle of vision chosen by the creator of the images and of the messages they are intended to convey, whether by choice of vantage point, weather, time of day, day of the week or time of year, in a place where the density, atmosphere and composition of the crowd at play varied dramatically in ways that could send sharply contrasting messages to a subsequent observer.[2] The temptation to view the Pleasure Beach's customers as an example of 'mass tourism', all effectively the same sort of people, exploited and manipulated by the providers of their mass-produced commercial entertainments and devoid of choice or agency on their own behalf, is tempting but misleading, and has to be resisted: we must remember that people could and did choose whether, when and how long to visit Blackpool and its Pleasure Beach, to decide which items of its extensive menu to try out or return to, and to work out for themselves what sensations they liked and why they liked them. But how people depicted the Pleasure Beach's customers, and for what audiences, are also important

1 http://www.culture.gov.uk/Cap/eip/eip_docs/blackpool/Blackpool_transcript.pdf pp. 44, evidence of Reg Haslam (referred to in transcript as Mr Haslem); 45–6, evidence of David Cam, accessed 19 May 2007; http://www.culture.gov.uk/Cap/eip/eip_docs/blackpool/post_info/BlackpoolCouncilLetter.pdf Chief Executive to Ms Valerie Curtis, 29 September 2006, p. 12, Tables 6 and 7, accessed 19 May 2007.

2 Colin Jacobson (ed.), *Underexposed* (London, 2002).

issues in their own right. We may be critical of what they said, wrote or represented as an indication of how people lived and what it meant to them, and we must remember that people reacted to these representations in different ways, from endorsement to indifference to angry rejection. But the depictions are important in their own right, not least for what they tell us about how some contemporaries thought about these things, and about the agenda of the media that distributed them.[3]

From an early stage the Pleasure Beach, like (for example) the Tower Ballroom or the Victoria Pier, was often seen as a democratic, accessible space where the classes mingled in the shared pursuit of innocent excitement. Even Blackpool's Edwardian Socialists, a marginalised minority in a town with little manufacturing industry or trade union organisation, were generally friendly towards the new amusement park. Most commentators from this background denounced the whole ethos of the Blackpool holiday, as had the Bolton socialist Allen Clarke in 1899. He blamed its high-pressure commercialism for luring working people into wasting their hard-earned savings on frivolities and amusements when they could have been virtuously enjoying the beauties of the countryside.[4] This was the normal reaction from the Independent Labour Party and similar quarters; but a few years later, after moving to Blackpool and becoming a publisher of Lancashire dialect guide-books, he became much friendlier towards the town and its amusements. As we saw in Chapter 2, the Pleasure Beach was, by 1907, '…a wonderful collection of entertainments aw i' th' open air – hobby horses, switchbacks, th' river caves, th' scenic railway, th' Spanish street, etc.'[5] Arthur Laycock, who in 1906 became Blackpool's first Socialist councillor, was happy to celebrate the Pleasure Beach in his own dialect writing, also on sale very cheaply to the holiday throng. Its rides were 'chep, gradely, grand' and 'lick owt i' creation, on sea or on land':

3 J. Golby and W. Purdue, *The Civilisation of the Crowd* (Stroud, 1999 edn.); S. Wright, 'Sun, sand, sea and self-expression', and J.K. Walton, 'British tourism between industrialisation and globalisation: an overview', in H. Berghoff, Barbara Korte, Ralf Schneider and Christopher Harvie (eds.), *The making of modern tourism: the cultural history of the British experience, 1600–2000* (London, 2002).

4 Allen Clarke, *The Effects of the Factory System* (Bolton, 1913, first published 1899).

5 (Allen Clarke), *Teddy Ashton's Gradely Guide to Blackpool* (4th edn., Blackpool, 1908), pp. 25, 30; and for context, Chris Waters, *British Socialists and the Politics of Popular Culture* 1884–1914 (Manchester, 1990; Harvey Taylor, *A Claim on the Countryside* (Keele, 1997); F. Trentmann, 'Civilization and its discontents: English neo-Romanticism and the transformation of anti-Modernism in twentieth-century Western culture', *Journal of Contemporary History* 29 (1994), pp. 586, 589.

**The mock-Classical entrance to the Velvet Coaster in 1908, when boardwalks still protected the customers from too much exposure to the sand. The oppressively heavy clothing worn in bright sunshine is characteristic of the time, although many younger women would promenade in white or pastel shades.**

Yo' may roam all o'er England
O'er th' wide world may seech
But yo'll find nowt that's grander
Than th' famed Pleasure Beach.
Talk abeawt fun an' frolic
An seets of aw sooarts!
There's no end to th' diversions
An' marlocks an' spooarts.

He also brought the sensations of the Pleasure Beach rides into his short stories. Two Lancashire working-class couples visit the amusement park, the young women 'donned up loike duchesses' and bent on combining laughter with the advancement of courtship. So Sally flirts with her Sam, teases him, clings to him on the rides, and kisses him in the darkness. The Velvet Coaster was 'like ridin' on rainbows on a streak o' greased lightenin''. On the Captive Flying Machine: 'Eh! It *were* a sensashun. My heart were i' my meauth, obbut for th'bit Sam held on to where he clutched mi' stays... risin' higher an' higher till I raly thowt we should knock th' bottom out o' th' clouds.' These early attempts to capture that combination of accessible

**Blackpool's pre-season municipal Carnivals of 1923 and 1924 brought additional visitors to the Pleasure Beach on what were normally working days. The special Carnival hats and bunting denote a special occasion, but the weather did not co-operate in creating the imagined Mediterranean atmosphere, and the faces do not suggest riotous mirth or a sense that everyday cares had been left behind or cast to the blustery winds.**

physical excitement and sexual intimacy that became a mainstay of the Pleasure Beach, and not just among its working-class customers, were published simply and unpretentiously for a popular market similar to those of the humorous dialect almanacs of the time, and helped to make a decent living for their author.[6]

Such attitudes were even more in evidence during the inter-war years, when a widespread assumption developed that all social classes were capable of enjoying the Pleasure Beach. When the local coroner presided over the inquest into the first fatality on the Big Dipper, in 1929, he told the jury that, 'We all know the Big Dipper… and I suppose everyone in this room has ridden on it. I have ridden on it several times myself.' This presumption of shared knowledge, bringing together the experiences of a supposed

6 *Fun on the Pleasure Beach wi' Sally an' Sam, Jimmy an' Jane Ann, Towd by Sally Hersel* (Blackpool, 1909), unpaginated; Cross and Walton, *Playful Crowd*, p. 81.

cross-section of Blackpool society, was not entirely innocent. It probably helped to guarantee an 'accidental death' verdict, exonerating the Pleasure Beach: the deceased was a railway dining car worker on an excursion from London, a stranger of no social standing who had brought about his own demise by standing up at the wrong point on the ride.[7] But it also reflected a frequently expressed idea of the inter-war years, that the Pleasure Beach was legitimately attractive to middle-class professionals in search of democratic fun, like the professors at the British Association meeting of 1936. Councillor W.R. Duckworth's remark in 1935, that 'it was significant that educationists and other visitors to Blackpool conferences often slipped away when the opportunity arose to experience the thrills of the Pleasure Beach', was a common perception, as was the reference to the cultured aristocracy at play that followed, with a reminiscence of the Earl of Crawford and Balcarres riding on the Big Dipper.[8]

When Frederick Cowles, author of (among other books) *The Magic of Cornwall* and *Pilgrim Ways*, agreed to write a book on the contrasting versions of England that could be visited from five major provincial cities, his explorations from Manchester inevitably brought him to Blackpool; and his encounter with the town and the Pleasure Beach of the mid-1930s celebrated the democratic vulgarity of the summer season from the perspective of a self-consciously tolerant but distant and condescending outside observer. In writing up his notes he seems to have confused the Pleasure Beach with parts of the 'Golden Mile', but the picture he paints of the amusement park is typical of the perceptions of many visiting writers in its combination of surprised enjoyment, and recognition of the unrestrained pleasure expressed by others, with a sense of guilt or unease at the necessary suspension of constraint, convention and detachment:[9]

> To many holiday-makers the Pleasure Beach is Blackpool. The greatest adventure they can imagine is a trip on the 'Big Dipper', and 'Noah's Ark' is the peak of real fun. The most amazing thing about the Pleasure Beach is that there is something for everybody. The quieter souls can float sedately through the 'River Caves' and visit, in the space of a few minutes, almost every country in the world. There are fortune-tellers galore, temples of mystery, scenic railways, shooting galleries, theatres of illusion, skittle-alleys, and pin-board saloons. All sorts of souvenirs can be carried away, from fantastic dolls to boxes of cheap chocolates, all legitimately won at games of skill... And into this bedlam, this topsy-turvy, fantastic

7 Pleasure Beach Archive, Cuttings Books, 1928–9, pp. 102–4.

8 Pleasure Beach Archive, Cuttings Books, 1935–6, p. 27.

9 Frederick I. Cowles, *Not far from the smoke* (London, 1935), pp. 58–60.

> fairground, I plunged. In the 'Noah's Ark' I yelled just as lustily as the others, and then, taking my courage in both hands, I braved the 'Big Dipper'. It is a thrilling experience. The car, carrying about twenty screaming people, mounts a steep gradient, and then suddenly hurls itself down again on the other side, and then up again just as quickly. The uncomfortable feeling that your middle has been left behind is liable to daunt timid souls. At the first dip the girls hold their breath, and at the second they hold the man who happens to be nearest. That, in Blackpool, is, I believe, quite a formal introduction, and many a happy romance has started on the 'Big Dipper'. I was glad when that perilous journey came to an end and I felt the good solid ground beneath my feet again. But a ride on the 'Big Dipper' is something that every Blackpool visitor should experience at least once... And such is pleasure! An hour on this fair-ground would land some people in a mental home, but to the majority it is the place where they can give their high spirits full rein.

Cowles communicates a sense of having encountered an alien culture, more communal and less constrained, more open to the spontaneous expression of feeling than the middle-class circles in which he usually moves; and he sums up the distinctive character of Blackpool, including the Pleasure Beach itself, as 'blatant vulgarity' of an exhausting and awe-inspiring kind.[10]

The novelist D.L. Murray, writing about the Blackpool of the 1930s in a tale published just after the Second World War, confirmed the Pleasure Beach's capacity for releasing inhibitions while offering an imagined description of a Big Dipper ride that sought to communicate the sensations and opportunities that it offered. Murray followed the common practice of treating the Pleasure Beach (and Blackpool) crowd as if it were a creature with a collective personality of its own, in this case an insect: '...the throng, which moved at caterpillar pace, loosening and coalescing again, laughing and calling to itself.'[11] William Holt used similar language in the *Daily Dispatch*, for example, viewing the crowds from the Tower: 'It is interesting to watch the streams of people crawling like flies. You can observe their mass habits, like insects.'[12] The novelist Frank Tilsley followed the same path: 'The promenade was thick with people. They came, following their wash and brush up, like flies clustering along a bar of Northpool's own rock.'[13] In similar vein, Murray referred to the carriages on the roller coasters as 'beetle-

10 Ibid., p. 61.
11 D.L. Murray, *Leading Lady* (London, 1947), p. 246.
12 William Holt, 'I Watch the North on Holiday', *Daily Dispatch*, 3 Aug. 1934, p. 12.
13 Frank Tilsley, *Pleasure Beach* (London, 1944), p. 31.

like'; but the description of the ride itself gave full weight to individual experiences within the crowd. But the people described are drawn from show business, a knowing and generally sophisticated group who register their distance from the 'ordinary' crowd even as they share its pleasures:[14]

> Abruptly they emerged into blinding daylight high above the world. They could glimpse the outskirts of Blackpool for a moment on a pale-green carpet; then their attention was frozen on to the track in front, going up and up and curling over at a point where it seemed to touch the clouds. The skeleton structure on which they were travelling was invisible beneath them, and Peter had a pricking in the soles of his feet at the sensation of being suspended in the midst of the firmament. The summit grew steadily nearer and nearer, while the car woke creaks from the wooden framework, and to Peter's nervous fancy shook alarmingly from side to side... The car as it glided over the top seemed to give a buck, while the gulf spread out below it, dotted with tiny booths, tents, the criss-cross of fences, and the black knots of the pleasure-hunters. Then, leaping at an instant into top speed, it hurled itself down the almost perpendicular incline, giving its passengers the feeling that their insides had been torn out and impaled upon the pinnacle they had left. To this was added, for Peter, the anguish of Gail's long, tinted nails digging into his flesh... Peter passed his arm around Gail's waist to hearten her... Even in his agony Peter thought that if Gail could learn to register terror in the theatre as she was doing now, they would pass her on to tragedy...

This passage brings out the thrilling aspects of the experience, conjuring up parallels with mountain paths and the view from an aeroplane window, and emphasizes the scope for erotic encounter (the central character recalls a previous ride in which the couple in front spent the whole time locked in a single kiss), while reminding the reader of less pleasant sensations (terror, giddiness, nausea) and bringing out the variety of responses in a small group (from placidly checking the racing pages during the ride to being physically sick at the end). What was pleasure and release for some was torture and pain for others, and there was a spectrum of mixed feelings. This is fiction, but clearly based on the author's reflection on past experiences and those of others, and as evidence it is no less valid (and perhaps no more difficult to use) than a direct first-hand account.

Other novelists dealing with inter-war Blackpool confirmed aspects of this picture while adding further dimensions. At J.L. Hodson's imagined Carnival of the mid-1920s (seen from the vantage point of 1937, and not

[14] Murray, *Leading Lady*, pp. 250–2.

firmly anchored in a particular year: the Big Dipper opened more than two months after the first Carnival in 1923), the Pleasure Beach in the evening became 'a centre of revelry – ardent flirtations took place on the Big Dipper and even on the Water-Chute', reinforcing a relationship between the Pleasure Beach and sexual encounter that might be continued or resumed later in the more conventionally romantic atmosphere of the ballrooms.[15] Frank Tilsley's 'Northpool' is presented as an amalgamation of the popular northern seaside resorts, but Blackpool is the dominant element, and the Pleasure Beach of its title is given the Blackpool name. Here, too, we have noise, crowds, euphoria and the release of inhibitions:[16]

> The sunny evening was filled with shrieks and laughter, the rattle of the machinery which animated the roundabouts and switchbacks, the crack of miniature rifles, the splash of water from the water-chute, the clamour of competing powerful-voiced showmen… Flushed and dishevelled young women hung limply on the arms of their escorts, vowing never again to go on that there Bowl Slide or Big Dipper or Flying Zig Zag. Young men wore imitation sailor hats which did not suit them, and carried, in an off-hand manner, trophies of the evening – cokernuts, Teddy Bears, velvet effigies of Snow-White… Their elation showed itself in uproarious laughter over nothing at all, in weird cat-calls and shrill whistling. They appeared to be a trifle drunk. The whole fairground appeared to be a trifle drunk, as though it were celebrating an event it was a little too tipsy exactly to recall.

Tilsley not only reminds us of the importance of the Pleasure Beach's own souvenir industry, consisting largely of trophies won on the stalls and sideshows that were such an important part of the whole experience. Through his central character, Tom Matthews, a coal miner taking a week's unofficial holiday from his Wigan pit, he also highlights the small-scale gambling that went with the shedding of everyday constraints and inhibitions, this time about budgets and money management in the prevailing atmosphere of 'spend money, spend money, spend money': '…On Pleasure Beach, you can put more pennies in a bigger variety of slots, than anywhere else in the country. Here, at least, folk know that money is not everything, that grubbing for money is not the be-all and end-all of a man's life… (Tom) was completely infected already by that holiday mania of people whose ordinary lives are ruled by mean economies; the mania to spend, spend, spend on everything, the more senselessly the better; to throw your

[15] J.L. Hodson, *Carnival at Blackport* (London, 1937), pp. 244–5.
[16] Tilsley, *Pleasure Beach*, p. 33.

money around with entire disregard for sense or value. He threw darts at playing cards, bull's eyes, paper hoops and even dart boards...'[17] Here was the fevered climax of the holiday year, as the accumulated, measured, disciplined savings of the previous fifty-one weeks were cast into the euphoric maelstrom of the crowded amusement park, where the 'folk' who knew that money was not everything were the customers rather than the management or concessionaires. It was all too easy to adopt a censorious, moralising or condescending tone when commenting on all this from the outside, and even when trying to understand it, especially in terms of an inappropriate language of 'mass' and 'masses'.[18]

Contemporary commentators could be equally condescending when trying to focus in on individual experiences within the crowd. In 1929 a reporter from Blackpool's own *West Lancashire Evening Gazette* offered to take a middle-aged male visitor on the Pleasure Beach for an hour. 'Bill' was described as having a worried air and a yellow straggling moustache, and wore a red and white tasselled beret as a concession to the frivolity associated with being in Blackpool. He 'walked as so many of Blackpool's visitors walk – slowly and with a ponderous deliberation which is so provoking to the town's men of Big Business.' His choice of amusement was undemanding: disdaining the thrill rides, he spent a long time throwing a ball at some boxes until he had won a canary, then played a horse racing game to win a red and white rabbit. After spending some time in a song promotion booth, and a few minutes watching the external show outside the Indian Temple of Mysteries, he concluded his hour in the reporter's care by watching with great interest 'the lady who makes the doughnuts', and eating some of her wares. His succinct verdict was that the Pleasure Beach was 'a grand fair'.[19] This is a reminder that many Pleasure Beach visitors took their pleasures slowly and phlegmatically, that associations with the travelling fairs of the industrial wakes and feasts died hard, and that the thrill rides and other excitements that tend to be celebrated by outsiders formed only part of a spectrum of attractions that had room for the quietest tastes. In the same year Hannen Swaffer captured this aspect of the Pleasure Beach crowd for the *Daily Express*: 'Thousands spend the day there. They move with a slow, smiling gait, unhurried, perfectly polite.'[20] In 1937 a Mass-Observation observer referred to people strolling about in a 'vague undirected way', and

17 Ibid., p. 19, 35.

18 P. Gurney, '"Intersex" and "Dirty Girls": Mass-Observation and working-class sexuality in England in the 1930s', *Journal of the History of Sexuality* 8 (1997), pp. 256–90.

19 Pleasure Beach Archive, Cuttings Books 1928–9, p. 130.

20 Ibid., p. 114.

**This crowd scene from the 1920s, looking northwards to the original Casino, seems at first to show a highly disciplined and orderly crowd, controlling its own traffic flows through the Pleasure Beach, until we realise that the photographer's presence has constructed the nature of the image, as most of the throng are gazing upwards at the camera; but this is still an impressive view of the Pleasure Beach at its busiest.**

for many people such relaxed behaviour was clearly part of the holiday, a perception that needs to be set alongside the assumption that Blackpool was always a high-pressure holiday environment.[21] On the eve of World War 2 S.P.B. Mais, a prolific (and culturally conservative) writer on travel and tourism themes, described Pleasure Beach customers as, '...by far the best-behaved and best-humoured crowd I have ever mingled with', reflecting the way they received in turn 'the best of good taste' from those who catered for them.[22]

Home movies, and a railway publicity film, from the 1920s and 1930s generally confirm this picture of respectable adults taking their pleasures slowly and sedately. This was neither a crowded nor a high-pressure environment. There are family parties and couples rather than large animated groups, with children concentrated into their own area of miniature rides, a few adults going bare-headed but most of them formally dressed in hats and suits. The still photographs from the Pleasure Beach collection endorse the dominance of respectability. Even where they do assemble larger crowds, their orderly image is enhanced by an orchestrated gaze at the camera, which gives the illusion of an orderly, regimented one-directional flow which would immediately fragment into counter-flows and eddies

[21] Mass-Observation Archive, W56/A, Blackpool June 1937, p. 5.
[22] Design History Archive, EMB54, *Great Thoughts*, August 1939.

without the invitation to pose. But the overwhelming impression is of relaxation, tranquillity and space rather than the frenetic pursuit of gratification against the clock in the limited time-span of the 'fifty-second week'. The only exception to the decorous norm is a film from 1929 which moves from revealing shots of female bathers at the South Shore pool to a sequence of prurient views of the legs and underwear of women sliding down the helter-skelter, with the women laughing and taking it in good part in a fairground or comic postcard spirit. But this is the only film of its kind in the collection.[23]

There were other ways of looking at the Pleasure Beach. When a Mass-Observation team arrived in Blackpool for the first time, in an expensive-looking Bentley that said a good deal about the social distance (and scope for misunderstanding) between some of the observers and the observed, a garage worker told them that they 'should go to the Pleasure Beach, and with the car we can get all the girls we want. He says that is the place where they go to be picked up by people who will and can spend money on them.'[24] Similar comments were often made about Coney Island, and the existence of such perceptions is interesting and important; but it would be hard to argue, not least from Mass-Observation's own reports on the sexual atmosphere of other parts of Blackpool, that the Pleasure Beach was particularly outstanding as a pick-up venue of this sort, or that the expectation of spending money involved the direct trade-off for sexual favours that is suggested here.[25]

The psychology of the Pleasure Beach also became a focus of interest in the 1930s. William Holt was not alone in becoming interested in this theme. On arrival at the Pleasure Beach he was curious about the 'piercing feminine screams, vibrating with horror and delight', and this led him straight into 'the bowels of the Noah's Ark', to investigate and describe the curious experiences that people found enjoyable in this setting: 'On South Shore I have had the exquisite pleasure of experiencing sudden draughts up my trouser legs and feeling the ground oscillate beneath my feet… I have been hit on the nose with weighing machines, and in eerie darkness, accompanied by a car-load of hysterical holiday-makers, amid peals of spooky laughter awful graves have opened, ghosts have jibbered (*sic*), skeletons have clutched at me, thin, invisible danglers have tickled my face.' Holt described the new Fun Palace as 'a good place for students of psychology

23 North West Film Archive, Manchester, Accessions Nos. 149, 152, 726, 754, 1169, 1822.

24 Mass-Observation Archive, W56/A, Blackpool, June 1937, p. 1; Gurney, '"Intersex" and "Dirty Girls"'.

25 Cross and Walton, *Playful Crowd*, pp. 69–70.

who want to know "why" people laugh when the floor gives way or when barrels appear to be falling on them, because here – after you have run the gauntlet yourself – you may sit down in comfortable tip-up chairs and watch the ordeals of those who follow. You may speculate on the causes, *a priori*, as to why men and women – especially women – love to be almost terrified to death when on their holidays.' But Holt outlined the possibilities for speculation without pursuing them any further himself: his subsequent encounter with the Pleasure Beach management produced no further enlightenment on this subject, as Leonard Thompson and his cohorts moved quickly into questions of accounting; and the suggested musings on the psychology of the amusement park customer had to be left to others.[26]

One of the speculators in this field was the psychologist Frank C. Thomas, who presented a paper on these issues at the British Association's Blackpool meeting in 1936, arguing that the Pleasure Beach offered a seductive combination of fear, security and curiosity. The rides were outside the customer's control, they did frightening and unpredictable things, but there was always the comforting certainty that escape would come at the last minute. The fear of the unknown was cross-cut by the curiosity to elucidate and explore it, and the Pleasure Beach provided controlled conditions for safe excitement. This analysis echoes, across a century and a half, the revaluations of seaside and mountainous environments as venues for managed and controlled excitement that helped to turn these hitherto dangerous and threatening locations into proper subjects of art and tourism at the dawn of the modern seaside holiday in the eighteenth century.[27]

This combination of sociological, cultural and scientific interest in the Pleasure Beach as a symbol of modern democratic leisure was not sustained after World War 2. During the post-war decades it tended to be absorbed into the more conventional working-class image of Blackpool as a whole, as the seaside holiday became open to almost everyone and the 'better classes' increasingly decamped to the Continent. An unpublished letter to the *Bolton Evening News* in November 1948, congratulating its editor on the paper's victory in a libel case against Bessie Braddock, the large, formidable, outspoken, working-class Labour MP for Liverpool Exchange, expressed widespread 'respectable' stereotypes about the post-war holiday crowds at Blackpool and elsewhere: 'I have seen a similar type (to Mrs Braddock) at Blackpool, at holiday times. A similar type of feature, full of food peculiar to the North: tripe, cowheel and black-pudding. All very happy and likeable.

26 William Holt, 'Merry Mirth-Makers at Blackpool', *Daily Dispatch*, 4 Aug. 1934, p. 6.

27 Pleasure Beach Archive, Cuttings Books, 1935–6, p. 129; A. Corbin, *The Lure of the Sea* (Cambridge, 1992).

But such a woman in the House of Commons, can only be imagined with horror.'[28] This political incarnation of a Donald McGill comic postcard stereotype was an example of exactly the kind of dominant image Thompson's Pleasure Beach had sought to keep at arm's length, even as it celebrated the democratic pleasures of its inclusive holiday throng. But the prevailing images began to shift again during the rising prosperity of the 1950s and early 1960s.

The McGill stereotypes were in steady decline from the 1950s onwards, although they could still be captured on camera along the Blackpool sea front a generation later. Even in the early twentieth century the resort's visiting public was already coming from far beyond its original Lancashire and West Yorkshire heartland, and the national market that was already being tapped in the 1930s was even more in evidence after the Second World War.[29] It was also arriving increasingly by coach, a process that had begun alongside still-expanding railway traffic during the 1920s and 1930s, and by car, as the balance really tipped from rail to road during the 1950s. In the mid-1960s the multi-tracked railway route past the Pleasure Beach to Central Station was cut short at Blackpool South, rapidly shrinking to a single-track branch line with an hourly local service; and the other main terminal at Blackpool North was set back to the old excursion station and lost many of its through services. These changes formed part of Dr Beeching's ill-advised programme of cuts in rail services in the mid-1960s, which not only reduced the ordinary services and snipped out sections of connecting lines along which holiday trains had been routed: it also did away with most of the excursion trains and their servicing facilities, reducing the effective capacity of the rail network still further.[30] When, in 1987, the Pleasure Beach at last obtained its own railway station, and British Rail agreed to provide all-in fares and books of tickets for the rides, such concessions had come to be of marginal importance. Since 1975 most visitors had come into town along the M55, which linked up with the national motorway network at Preston; and a new direct access route to the town centre opened in 1986, making vast areas of car parking available along the line of the old railway route. By this time 80 per cent of people interviewed in the English Midlands had been to the Pleasure Beach at least once and thirty

[28] Frank J. Staff to *Bolton Evening News*, 11 November 1948, Bolton Archives, *Evening News* collection, by courtesy of Janet McLarney.

[29] Walton, thesis, p. 267, Table 5.4; J.K. Walton, 'The world's first working-class seaside resort? Blackpool revisited, 1840–1974', *Transactions of the Lancashire and Cheshire Antiquarian Society* 88 (1992), 1–30.

[30] B. McLoughlin, *Blackpool and the Fylde: 150 Years of Railways* (Wadenhoe, 1996).

per cent had been at least seven times. The numbers of Irish visitors, and of British Asians, were beginning to grow, as were those from Saudi Arabia and other Gulf states, encouraged by commercial links with British Aerospace at nearby Warton.[31]

The visitor profile was changing in other important ways: between 1972 and 1992 the proportion of Blackpool visitors between 15 and 34 years of age had grown from 20 to 43 per cent, and this could only be to the Pleasure Beach's benefit, as it complemented the pubs, clubs and 'stags and hens' parties that were making Blackpool a destination of choice for the hedonistic young.[32] A further new development that was becoming visible in the early 1990s, however, was the emergence of Blackpool as a holiday destination for young British Muslims, especially from Lancashire and southern Scotland, celebrating Eid ul-Fitr and Eid ul-Adha. A Halal fast food outlet opened on Ocean Boulevard to cater for this new market. As these festivals move through the year following the lunar calendar, the Pleasure Beach began to open specially out of season to meet this demand, which was sometimes associated with display and excess among young Muslims which attracted severe criticism from some commentators within the culture.[33]

The Pleasure Beach coped effectively with changing traffic flows and visiting publics. In 1966 praise came from a *Guardian* reader based in Teddington, Middlesex, who was impressed by the Pleasure Beach's cleanliness as compared with the 'third rate and dirty' Battersea fun fair, and by 'the many ultra modern ideas for amusement' which were 'all value for money.'[34] In the same year the satirist John Wells, going deliberately against the grain of his readers' expected assumptions, offered affectionate praise for Blackpool at party conference time in the *Spectator*, presenting the Pleasure Beach to his Conservative readers as 'a mass of vulgar delights that seem to have disappeared from less enterprising places of entertainment'. He particularly liked the lugubrious litter-eating lion outside the Noah's Ark.[35] This combination of nostalgia, modernity, respectability and vulgarity as bases

31 Bennett, *Century of Fun*, pp. 119–20.
32 Ibid., p. 129.
33 http://artsweb.bham.ac.uk/bmms/1993/03March1993.html accessed 7 Oct. 2006; www.en.wikipedia.org/wiki/Blackpool_Pleasure_Beach accessed 7 Oct. 2006; I.H. Ali, 'What are you going to do on Eid?', http://risingcrescent.com/Mambo/index.php?option=com_content&task=view&id=Jb&Hemid=1 accessed 7 Oct. 2006; K. Qureshi, 'Trans-bonding spaces: Scottish Pakistanis and trans-local/national identities', *International Journal of Cultural Studies* 9 (2006), pp. 207–28.
34 Pleasure Beach Archive, Cuttings Books, 1953–69, *Guardian*, 28 Sept. 1966.
35 Ibid., *Spectator*, 14 Oct. 1966.

**By the 1970s the carefully-constructed orderliness of the Pleasure Beach was beginning to fray at the edges. Litter is now in evidence, and informality has shaded over into scruffiness.**

for approval suggested that the Pleasure Beach was continuing to have the best of all worlds in the eyes of a cross-section of visitors; and in 1969 Leonard Thompson laid claim to another virtuous circle, commenting that in relatively hard times the amusement park benefited from a switch from foreign to domestic holidays, while in good times the regular visitors had more money to spend. According to David Robson, the Pleasure Beach was 'quite simply the only mind-blowing amusement park in Britain', in a Blackpool that was still 'the home of good clean fun'.[36]

At this very point, however, media reports of violence and disorder at the Pleasure Beach began to multiply. During the 1966 Illuminations a Glasgow youth stabbed a Bradford teenager who was visiting the Pleasure Beach on a youth club outing, at about the same time as a similar case at Diamond Lil's.[37] Even more disturbing were fights between large groups of (mainly) young men representing aggressive new youth cultures. Blackpool had escaped the 'Mods and Rockers' troubles of the mid-1960s, but a few

36 Ibid., *Financial Times*, 23 May 1969, and undated newspaper cutting, c. 1971.
37 Ibid., unidentified cutting, 28 Oct. 1966, and undated, unidentified cutting.

years later battles like the one involving around thirty skinheads and six 'long-haired youths', with participants from Salford, Scunthorpe and Bolton, or the occasion when eleven 'leather-jacketed young people ran amok in the Pleasure Beach', shouting their intention to 'get the skins', were potentially very damaging to the amusement park's carefully nurtured image of family-friendly, classless respectability.[38] Worse still were the invasions by groups of visiting football 'hooligans', which affected much of the town centre and south promenade. Two hundred followers of Stoke City, 'mainly' skinheads, caused a major disturbance on the Pleasure Beach after a match, but the most dramatic stories concerned Manchester United, whose 800 visiting 'hooligan' fans were fearsome enough by reputation to cause an angry and horrified Leonard Thompson to close the amusement park pre-emptively against the threat of vandalism and violence. This was more a matter of teenage intimidation than of serious crime, but it acted as a deterrent to respectable visitors and a loss of reputation and revenue, although the successive relegations of Blackpool Football Club to the second (1971) and third (1978) tiers of English professional football reduced the scale of the problem.[39] But these disturbing developments were part of a shift during the late twentieth century towards a younger and more assertive visiting public, although this was a matter of emphasis, and to some extent one of selective reporting, rather than a total transformation; and the pathological elements reported here were only part of this story.

Some visitors to Blackpool took little or no interest in the Pleasure Beach. The self-published Blackpool holiday diaries of Jimmy Campbell, a constant visitor through the post-war generations, mention almost every conceivable entertainment venue, from the Winter Gardens to the Sandcastle by way of the Golden Mile, the parks and the churches, but apart from the Ice Drome he says nothing about the Pleasure Beach between a comment on post-war barbed wire and desolation after the end of the season in October 1946 and a visit in June 1988, just before the opening of the Avalanche, although his remarks on changes to the names of food outlets suggest unmentioned visits in the interim.[40] This is a reminder that however important the Pleasure Beach was becoming to Blackpool's post-war economy and identity, it was still one attraction among many, although Campbell's low-key commentaries also provide prosaic and sporadic illumination of the declining range and scope of what was on offer, from the sad decline of the North Shore paddling pool to the departure of the town's

[38] Ibid., unidentified cutting, early 1970s, and *West Lancashire Evening Gazette*, 25 Oct. 1971.
[39] Ibid., 1969–74, unidentified cuttings, c. 1970.
[40] Jimmy Campbell, *Tower Above All* (Upton-on-Severn, 1991), pp. 23, 131–2.

Rugby League club. As other outdoor pleasures faded, the Pleasure Beach stood out all the more strongly for its continuing capacity to innovate and to pull in crowds who wanted something new and exciting alongside 'more of the same'. Campbell's lack of interest was a reminder that the Pleasure Beach's appeal was not universal; but there were plenty of takers for a menu of attractions whose staple fare could be returned to, but with something new every year to excite and titillate.

At the other extreme, of course, the Pleasure Beach catered for the obsessive roller-coaster buffs who wanted to experience as many rides as possible, to compare and discuss them, and in some cases to set endurance records. In the process some of them generated meticulously compiled websites of considerable value to historians. The vogue, particularly among American visitors, for 'collecting' the Pleasure Beach's 'Woodies' was already becoming visible in the 1980s, and in 1985 the American Roller Coaster Enthusiasts brought their conference to the Blackpool amusement park for the first time.[41] Coaster marathons began in the late 1960s, and Richard Rodriguez, a history teacher from New York and doctoral candidate in educational psychology at Chicago's Loyola University, brought them to Blackpool in 1979, 1980 and 1994 as he pursued successive world endurance records on the Big Dipper, the last one in conjunction with the opening of the Big One. In 1998, when he returned to ride it for 1000 hours, Geoffrey Thompson was eager to urge him to try 2000 hours in 2000. It was all excellent publicity.[42]

But in 1999 Natacha Henry of *Le Monde Diplomatique* suggested that for most visitors the Pleasure Beach was 'considered to be principally a place for a stroll with the family, eventually giving way to temptation and opening the wallet' to enjoy a ride or two.[43] It has even come to be seen as a suitable venue for educational visits by school parties: the Pleasure Beach provides an introductory presentation, the older rides are used to make the point that part of the site's appeal is as a working museum of amusement park technology, and staff are warned to be careful not to lose their dignity completely on the more challenging rides, although they are also alerted that the Ice Show's costumes may be 'too racy for a school trip.'[44] Crowded as it was, with a tremendous variety of rides intersecting excitingly in a confined space, the Pleasure Beach at the turn of the millennium was certainly

41 Bennett, *Century of Fun*, p. 119.

42 Martin, 'The Rollercoaster Champion of the World'; Bennett, *Century of Fun*, pp. 135–6.

43 Natacha Henry, 'A Blackpool la classe operaia va ancora in paradiso', *Le Monde Diplomatique*, Luglio 1999, p. 13.

44 http://www.rogerfrost.com/the.htm accessed 21 Aug. 2006.

not as high-pressure a visitor experience as Eurodisney, which was by this time the only European theme park to claim more visitors in a year.

But just as Disney can appal as well as appeal, the Pleasure Beach in the late twentieth century (like much of the rest of Blackpool's popular pleasure industry) began to dismay and repel outside observers, as the sort of journalistic attacks that had long been levelled at Blackpool's accommodation industry were extended across the resort. The novelist and polemicist Auberon Waugh, writing in the *Sunday Telegraph* from a position of obvious ignorance and prejudice, offered an early example of intemperate denunciation in 1981, drawing an angry response from Geoffrey Thompson on the letters page. Thompson pointed out that, 'Light, laughter and fun are indeed what Blackpool provides, for those adult enough not to fear being seen to enjoy them', and he urged Waugh to try the sophistication of the Pleasure Beach's *Viva Hollywood* show and the food in the Casino's White Tower restaurant.[45] In less polemical vein Christopher Somerville, touring the British coast in the late 1980s, came away with mixed but predominantly negative impressions. Somerville is often unreliable on details; but the overall picture of the Pleasure Beach as a 'heartless whirlpool', many of whose 'seriously frightening' rides were the last hope of a Blackpool in serious overall decline, was amplified and developed in other critical commentaries towards the end of the twentieth century: 'Here, as along all Blackpool's seafront, things are just as they have always been, only more so... It's a riotous teenagers' paradise *par excellence*, but toddlers come here, too, for a rainy afternoon's roundabouting, and so do mob-handed factory outings for a chicken dinner and a rude show. Through the fog of sensation so aggressively spread around the Pleasure Beach a few details stand out – the nerve-scraping irritation of the manic maniacal laughter from outside the Fun House; the all-pervading hot sweet scent of candy-floss; the rapt faces of children queuing for the most terrifying rides...'[46] The emphasis on teenagers illustrated some of the changes of the late twentieth century, as the focus of much commentary shifted from families and a mix of ages to teenagers and young adults, and from the sedate to the lively, noisy and even rowdy; and an increasing proportion of published opinion from outside the culture was negative.[47] But at the beginning of the twenty-first century Iain Aitch provided a more balanced commentary, with revealing awareness of context, comparing the Pleasure Beach favourably with the rest of tourist Blackpool in the process: 'Because of its relative sobriety, the Pleasure Beach

45 Pleasure Beach Archive, Geoffrey Thompson to *Sunday Telegraph*, 15 Sept. 1981.

46 Christopher Somerville, *Britain Beside the Sea* (London, 1989), pp. 215–6.

47 See above, Chapter 1.

had a different atmosphere to the seafront. There were far more families, couples, young teens and even some of Blackpool's older visitors... These days the Pleasure Beach is far closer to the theme parks of Alton Towers and Thorpe Park than the fairgrounds of old... But... the free admission policy (you buy tickets or wristbands to ride) and the sheer concentration of rides and amusements does still allow for atmosphere where the theme parks have only sanitised, officially sanctioned "fun".'[48]

As this demonstrates, Andrew Martin (as cited in Chapter 1) is far from being the only positive voice. Rachel Campbell-Johnston, writing in the *Times* in October 2000, was all in favour of Blackpool as a student and post-student destination for 'a whole generation who can't quite face maturity', which has 'achieved a sort of post-modern hip, more a sensation safari than a traditional seaside holiday' and spends most of its time at Blackpool enjoying the Pleasure Beach rides and laughingly comparing notes about them. Here was an important new market for the Pleasure Beach at the turn of the millennium.[49] Overlapping with this perception is that of Paul Flynn in 2004, writing with up-to-date nostalgia from a more 'traditional' visitor background about the Pleasure Beach crowd's appealing combination of threatening appearance and (generally) relaxed reality, as 'the democratising effect of a rollercoaster turns the most ardent tyke into a pussycat' in surroundings that combine 'spectacularly terrifying' novelties with the reassuring presence of the 'battered old rust-buckets' of yesteryear. The Pleasure Beach's continuing ability to captivate and recruit new generations, using nostalgia as well as novelty, is captured by these remarks.[50]

The Pleasure Beach workforce was central to the visitor experience. It was the intermediary between the technology of the rides and the needs and desires of these changing visiting publics, and its satisfactory performance was essential to minimising adverse comments among those who reported on the experience. It was divided between a core of year-round, permanent workers, a significant group of summer regulars who returned season after season, and a penumbra of casuals who came and went irregularly for shorter periods. The Pleasure Beach soon became one of Blackpool's biggest employers, with 600 workers at the height of the season in 1914, well over 1000 in the inter-war years, and around 2000 during the last thirty years of the twentieth century, including 200 permanent maintenance staff among a growing establishment at the turn of the millennium.[51]

48 Iain Aitch, *A Fete Worse than Death* (London, 2003), p. 166.
49 *The Times*, 7 Oct. 2000, 'Travel', p. 6.
50 Paul Flynn, 'Why I love Blackpool Pleasure Beach', *Guardian* G2, 26 Feb. 2004, p. 23.
51 Pleasure Beach Archive, Cuttings Books, 1969–74, undated article by Geoffrey Mather.

Levels of skill among the permanent workforce were often high, although not always formally obtained or recognised. When Leonard Thompson addressed the British Association in 1936, he emphasized the sheer range and scope of Pleasure Beach maintenance staff skills and competences. Their work included, 'Repair and maintenance of all plant; surveying, levelling and draughtsmanship; electrical engineering from motive power to decorative schemes of illumination; gas and water services; making roads, bridges and tunnels – even making ice cream in our own factory...' But he also recognised their limitations, while praising their versatility in other respects. The Pleasure Beach used wood extensively in its constructions not only because it was cheaper, but because it was 'more easily worked by their own labour, many of whom were carpenters (although in the summer season they might be boatmen, engine drivers, Grand National jockeys, skating instructors and such like).' This was jocular in tone, but it also reflected some of the ways in which the Pleasure Beach benefited from the Blackpool economy, with its seasonal fluctuations that provided cheap labour when the Pleasure Beach most needed it, and its floating population of skilled workers who lived mainly by the accommodation industry and welcomed any opportunity to deploy their skills in a tight labour market, in which 'most seasonal workers are that by necessity rather than choice'.[52]

The Pleasure Beach's demand for labour fluctuated widely. Extra workers often had to be taken on for special jobs, as when new rides were installed by Pleasure Beach staff. In late September 1934, for example, 200 men were already working double shifts on the building of the new Grand National.[53] Seasonal fluctuations imposed long hours as well as versatility for established Pleasure Beach workers, including performers. In 1929 the pianist at the Indian Pavilion might play accompaniments from 10 a.m. through to 10.30 p.m. at busy times, with only a few short breaks, playing anything 'from Bach to Horatio Nichols'.[54] Small compensations might include a discount at the cafes that stayed open beyond midnight and catered for amusement workers at 50 per cent less than the normal price.[55] But for many workers, especially those outside the core of permanent employees, a combination of low pay and opportunities for petty fiddling created a climate of suspicion which led to the intermittent imposition of strict security regimes and ready recourse to the courts over and above the

52 Design History Archive, EMB54, *West Lancashire Evening Gazette*, 10 Sept. 1936; K. Neal and J. Edwards, *Seasonal Unemployment in Blackpool* (Blackpool, 1950), p. 10.

53 Design History Archive, EMB19, *Daily Dispatch*, 19 Sept. 1934.

54 Pleasure Beach Archive, Cuttings Books, 1928–9, p. 122.

55 Mass-Observation Archive, W56/A, Blackpool, June 1937, p. 44.

**The construction team for the Virginia Reel installation, shortly after the First World War. An unusual opportunity to look at the workers 'behind the scenes' who were essential to the creation and functioning of the whole enterprise.**

sanction of dismissal. In 1957 the *Daily Herald* published an exposé of the wages and working conditions of Pleasure Beach seasonal workers, finding a group of six pensioners in their late sixties and early seventies who were allegedly working a 67-hour week for between £7.50 and £8.50, with one day off and a 2 p.m. start on Sundays. Younger men worked longer hours for just under £9 per week, and female cashiers who worked in their boxes for eight hours at a stretch without relief received an average of £5.50. There were no staff toilets and no staff canteen, and complaints were stifled by the threat of the sack, as there were plenty of other takers for the work. 'Snoopers' were a further grievance: 'They complain that they are checked, double-checked and can be sacked at a minute's notice.' This was effectively a non-union workplace: the General and Municipal Workers had recruited some members in the mid-1950s after helping to settle a pay dispute, but most of them had let their membership lapse, apparently because they feared the loss of their jobs. The Pleasure Beach management refused to make any detailed comment, although it might have made the point that the ample supply of labour at these rates and under these conditions suggested that there were many worse workplaces in a Blackpool where the enormous supply of seasonal migrant labour always threatened to outweigh the demand, and where small, non-union workplaces with very informal hiring and firing customs were the norm.[56]

56 Pleasure Beach Archive, Cuttings Books, 1953–69, *Daily Herald*, 21 Aug. 1957.

A series of court cases during the 1960s suggested that the Pleasure Beach in the later years of the Leonard Thompson era was at times an authoritarian employer, willing to invoke the law to reinforce the sanction of dismissal for petty frauds and thefts, and reluctant to recognise external constraints on its own behaviour as an employer. Its complaints about Selective Employment Tax, the discriminatory tax levelled against employment in service industries as the Wilson government sought to encourage manufacturing, between 1966 and the new Heath government's repeal of the measure in 1971, were convincing. The entertaining revelation that (ironically) the Pleasure Beach's candy floss vendor was the only employee to be exempt from SET, because he manufactured the tangible product that he sold, was a good illustration of the absurdity of the tax, which was part of a long saga of discrimination against and failure to recognise the importance of the leisure and tourist industries in Britain. The tax also worked in such a way as to prevent the employment of part-time temporary pensioners, who had been an important source of cheap and (in effect) subsidised labour during the season.[57] The fate of two 63-year-old gardener's labourers who were dismissed in 1967 when the Pleasure Beach reduced its winter staff, however, suggests a rather cavalier attitude to labour laws. The Pleasure Beach management presented a written statement to the resulting Industrial Tribunal, but provided no representation at the hearing, and was unable to substantiate a story that one of the men had received and rejected a verbal offer of alternative employment at the Ice Drome. The men won their case and were awarded redundancy pay. The company's lack of record-keeping and failure to observe standard legal and Industrial Tribunal procedures painted a picture of authoritarianism and administrative carelessness which found endorsement in other workplace conflicts during this period.[58]

The 1960s saw a series of prosecutions of Pleasure Beach employees for petty theft and fraud, under circumstances that suggested that a lax management regime had provided temptations which helped to explain, though not to excuse, the offences. In 1968 two attendants on the Turnpike, young men aged 18 and 20, were each fined £25 for collecting the fares for a repeat ride and pocketing the money. This echoed an earlier case in 1962, when the Pleasure Beach called in detectives and suspended four workers over a similar allegation of keeping the money from repeat rides; and in 1971 a woman of 54 and a 20-year-old man were given conditional discharges for stealing 30p from the company by allowing two boys to ride

57 Ibid., *Yorkshire Evening Press*, 15 June 1968; *Lancashire Evening Post*, 14 June 1968.
58 Ibid., *West Lancashire Evening Gazette*, 7 March 1967.

without payment. Another similar case in about 1970 saw a boat ride attendant let customers in through a side entrance and keep the money, and in a separate case a ticket collector admitted people to his ride via the exit, charging them 5p per head. He was already subject to a suspended sentence of six months for theft, and was sentenced to a further six months to run consecutively. Additional evidence in these cases included a claim that the defendant 'was hungry and had no money', while the 54-year-old offender was a widow who had worked for the company for nine years and was paid £10 per week for a 6-day working week of about 78 hours.[59] Further cases around 1970 included two young men who received conditional discharges for stealing and handling a small quantity of crockery and glasses from the company when one of them was working temporarily as a cook, and a 35-year-old woman who absconded with £22 of takings after working for two days as a cashier. She gave a Blackburn address when eventually prosecuted, and explained that she had nowhere for herself and family to live, and the money was too much of a temptation.[60] All this suggests that the Pleasure Beach sometimes employed casual labour of no fixed abode and sometimes of uncertain honesty in jobs that involved handling money, that it paid such people low wages for long hours, that its systems of financial control had loopholes that proved difficult to close, and that it responded to the problems of petty theft, embezzlement and sometimes organised fraud that resulted from this situation by occasional tightening of surveillance and routine recourse to the courts to punish small offenders as a warning to others. We cannot tell whether the sudden rash of such occurrences recorded in the newspaper cuttings books around 1970 was the product of new record-keeping practices, or whether it reflected a genuine upsurge in dishonesty or the use of the courts, but it gives pause for thought about the nature of labour relations in a workforce containing large numbers of footloose casual workers, including students, towards the end of the Leonard Thompson regime, and perhaps afterwards.[61]

We have a couple of reminiscences of working on or for the Pleasure Beach in the late twentieth century to put some flesh on these bones. Ian Beech worked on the Virginia Reel during its last years between 1979 and 1982 as an employee of Green Star, a member of the Border Television

59 Ibid., *West Lancashire Evening Gazette*, 26 July 1968; *Daily Mail*, 20 Oct. 1962; 1969–74, two unidentified cuttings, no date, c. 1970 and Summer 1971.

60 Pleasure Beach Archive, Cuttings Books, 1969–74, unidentified cuttings, no date, *c.* 1970 and 1972.

61 Ibid., unidentified cutting (female cashier electrocuted while taking a short cut, no date, *c.* 1970).

group of companies that actually operated the ride, and he also worked directly for the Pleasure Beach itself, helping to operate five rides for Green Star and twelve for the Pleasure Beach. On the Reel he was officially an electrician, maintaining the drive motors but also walking the track to look for damage and loose bolts. On other rides he also had to be versatile, but reckoned the level of skill required to be variable, with some being needed on the Turtle Chase but the Cable Way being more notable for requiring 'a lot of walking'. As Geoffrey Mather commented around 1970, Pleasure Beach workers might 'walk 25 miles in a working day and not notice.' During the season the hours were long, starting by walking the track at 9 a.m. and working through to midnight without a break on busy Illuminations week-ends. Morale was sustained by a rough camaraderie expressed through practical jokes, which included the fixing of a dead rat at eye level in a tool cupboard, with a cigarette placed in its teeth, to frighten the most squeamish member of the team. During the winter on the Reel the cars were stripped down, and the bearings were replaced and repacked. Beech clearly had a sense of pride in work and was interested enough not only to provide an extensive retrospective interview for an enthusiasts' website, but also to speculate on the motives for abandoning the Reel (a structural survey requiring too much renovation work on what had become a 'rough' ride) and to comment on what he saw as management's unsentimental attitude towards the rides, which were fine for just as long as they turned a profit. This is a reminder of the importance of the Pleasure Beach's core of regular, experienced workers, people who thought about the job as they learned while doing it, and were anything but rootless or unskilled. Without this kind of workforce the whole enterprise would, literally, have collapsed.[62]

On the other hand, the long-serving workers might enjoy telling tales that illustrated the shortcomings of their less efficient or reputable colleagues. Thus Brian McCormick, who had risen to be Park Office Administration Manager at the beginning of the new millennium, shared the story of the 'little old lady' who worked as cashier on a ride and displayed a sign asking for 5p more than the official Pleasure Beach price, pocketing the difference until someone in authority noticed. This fitted in with the string of similar offences that were recorded among the Pleasure Beach press cuttings around 1970. He also reminisced about an operator of the Monorail who, at the enforced end of his brief tenure of the job, allowed

[62] http://www.themagiceye.co.uk/reel.html accessed 1 Aug. 2006; Pleasure Beach Archive, Cuttings Books, 1969–74, undated article by Geoffrey Mather, c. 1970.

two trains to collide because 'I was reading the Argos catalogue'; and he added to the store of practical joke stories with the tale of a colleague who waded into the water on the Tom Sawyer ride to confiscate some illicit beer from a customer, and was advised to dry off by standing on the edge of a circular rotating platform with his arms and legs extended, until he realised that this public humiliation was neither an enforceable instruction nor a serious suggestion.[63]

The Pleasure Beach continued to employ a core of permanent staff and a fluctuating seasonal workforce throughout the post-war period, coming and going according to rhythms of varying regularity. The comparative advantage of working in wood declined as new materials and technologies came to the fore, and the permanent staff became even more versatile. The company took more and more aspects of the amusement park's business under its own direct control, as the role of concessions continued to diminish. By the early 1980s concessionaires dealt with only 5 per cent of food and drink sales and operated only three of 84 rides; and by 1993 all the catering was done in-house. The concessionaires' last redoubt was the slot machine arcades, most of which were brought under direct Pleasure Beach management during the 1990s.[64] This meant that the Pleasure Beach company itself was becoming steadily more important as a direct employer within the park, and by the 1980s it was beginning to improve conditions for its full-time workers in a traditional paternalist style. A new 'diner and social club' for staff opened in 1980, and in 1986 the company was quick to take up a national profit-sharing scheme, distributing ten per cent of profits among the permanent staff after a threshold of a million pounds had been passed. Around 190 employees benefited during the first three years, indicating the size of the established workforce. By 1993 it had increased to 224, although a year later the number had fallen back to 212.[65] The number of permanent staff then seems to have grown considerably, perhaps in response to the lengthening of the season as week-ends became busy for most of the year while the old-style July and August peak withered and died. In 2006, however, press reports on fears of job losses after an 'efficiency review' commissioned from a consultant estimated that there were 400 permanent members of staff, of whom, on one contested estimate, 70 were said to be at risk. Strong indications of unease and mistrust among the work-

63 http://www.themagiceye.co.uk ARKive Part 2, interview with Brian McCormick, accessed 1 Aug. 2006.

64 Bennett, *Century of Fun*, pp. 118, 129–30. It is impossible to extract precise trends from the section on p. 118.

65 Ibid., pp. 120, 129, 139.

force, which was a dangerous new development, thus appeared at a point when the head of Public Relations' use of the language of a 'stronger, fitter Pleasure Beach' seemed somewhat at odds with her reassurance that this was a family business whose workforce was being kept fully in the picture. Meanwhile claims that the Pleasure Beach was employing 'several hundred eastern Europeans, principally Polish workers' during the season went unchallenged at the Casino enquiry.[66]

This suggests that the Pleasure Beach's relationship with its workforce was normally similar to that with its rides, as described by Ian Beech: it was fine so long as they accepted the wages and working conditions, worked efficiently and did not cause problems. The development of profit-sharing schemes in the 1980s and 1990s was entirely compatible with the company's long-standing suspicion of government interference and external regulation: this was a voluntary measure, opting in to an Act of Parliament to benefit long-serving permanent staff. The enterprise depended for its profitability on keeping up with, and indeed anticipating, the desires of its predominantly (but never exclusively) working-class clientele, and sustaining the sort of atmosphere that mingled security and excitement, the familiar and the outlandish, at acceptable prices through periods of inflation and enhanced competition (especially in the 1970s and 1980s). To do this it needed to invest heavily in the installation and maintenance of expensive machinery which took at least ten years to recoup the initial costs. This inevitably put pressure on wages and labour conditions in a local economy in which the supply of seasonal labour tended to outrun the demand, pushing down on wages and working conditions. When we look at the Pleasure Beach's customers and workers together, and at the relationships between their needs and aspirations, we see that the satisfaction of the customers, and the continuing viability of the enterprise, was founded on the payment of low wages for seasonal workers with minimum security or overheads. This should not surprise us. Further comment on the wider social, cultural and economic significance of the Pleasure Beach over the 'long' twentieth century, within Blackpool and beyond it, follows in the final chapter.

65 www.blackpooltoday.co.uk for 17 Aug. 2006, accessed 21 Aug. 2006; http://www.culture.gov.uk/Cap/eip/eip_docs/blackpool/Blackpool_transcript.pdf p. 41, evidence of Michael Edwards, p. 41.

# 6 The Pleasure Beach and the Wider World

'The immense Pleasure Beach provides the ultimate in calculated thrills.'[1] This comment of 1959, in a book that was intended to attract and guide visitors to Britain from overseas, is remarkable for encapsulating the core of the Pleasure Beach's reputation, nature and identity. It was not 'immense', at least in size, though tightly packed and visually very busy. But its thrills were certainly carefully calculated, and none the less thrilling for that, while the promise to provide 'the ultimate' in accessible excitement was essential to the stories the Pleasure Beach told about itself. Moreover, this claim was made (in what was supposed to be an 'objective' source) at a point when the amusement park's delayed recovery from the Second World War was only just beginning, Joseph Emberton had recently died, and the great Thompson and Emberton project of the modernist 1930s was visibly in need of refreshment. It therefore paid a particularly impressive tribute to the lasting spell that the Pleasure Beach had cast over the idea of the amusement park in Britain and beyond, at precisely the point where new challenges were about to emerge in the form of new kinds of theme park and of alternative holiday styles and destinations, and when the Pleasure Beach itself was about to set under way a long new cycle of innovation and investment. Enthusiastic appraisals of this sort invite more extended and comparative attempts to assess size, scale and significance. What did the rise and successive transformations of the Pleasure Beach contribute, over a century or so, to Blackpool, the seaside, Britain and the wider world?

We begin with Blackpool. As befitted its location at the southern end of the world's first working-class seaside resort, the Pleasure Beach was the first British seaside amusement park of its kind, though it owed a great deal to metropolitan and provincial precursors like Vauxhall and Belle Vue, and to seaside resort pleasure gardens like Margate's Dandelion and Blackpool's own Raikes Hall. As we saw in Chapter 1, it emerged in parallel with the great Coney Island amusement parks in the north-eastern United States, and stood at the forefront of a rapid Edwardian proliferation of seaside amusement parks in Britain, notably on the Irish Sea at Southport and Morecambe, but right across the coastlines of the rest of England and Wales from Whitley Bay in the north-east to Southend and Margate on the

1 G. Douglas Bolton, *Presenting Britain* (Edinburgh and London, 1959), p. 92.

**The Voyage in a Submarine was a classic early Pleasure Beach attraction, offering an 'educational' simulation of an inaccessible, novel and dangerous kind of experience, embellished by the imagined drama of divers fighting as well as working, and feeding into a patriotic admiration for all things naval and military as international tensions mounted before the First World War.**

Thames estuary, and Porthcawl and Barry Island in South Wales. But these developments in the popular resorts (or, as in Southport, on the 'popular' side of more 'select' ones), formed part of an Edwardian revolution in popular entertainment and amusement technology which applied electricity to the generation of new kinds of thrills, illusions and visual delights to create new kinds of spectacle and of thrilling experience for the playful but increasingly restrained and 'civilised' crowds of 'industrial saturnalia'. It began to transform the attractions of the travelling fairs that continued to punctuate the pleasure calendar of towns and villages throughout England, but it was in the more permanent and increasingly 'respectable' setting of the seaside amusement park that they were able to unite the disciplined industrial working class with their 'betters' in pursuit of commercial pleasure, in a new 'mass' entertainment market which actually brought together a rainbow array of people and cultures in pursuit of similar kinds of hedonistic excitement in their limited free time. The people who made up these crowds combined a relaxation of the disciplines, routines and constraints of everyday life, stimulated by the novel sensations of the rides and shows themselves and the urge to spend a year's accumulation of holiday savings, with an inescapable concern for respectability and for what neighbours and workmates, who were also on holiday in the same places, might think. This was 'carnivalesque' in its celebration of excess in eating and drinking, and its temporary repudiation of everyday caution, thrift and constraint; but this was a circumscribed carnival, muted (as were all 'traditional' carnivals) by the knowledge that other eyes were watching, that work awaited on the Monday, and that the rent would have to be paid. It was also modern, indeed up-to-date, in its dependence on industrial machinery in every sense, from the technology of the rides themselves in this 'pleasure factory', to the systems of factory holidays, accommodation and transport services which enabled the customers to arrive, stay beyond a day and pay the going rate for their enjoyment.[2] By the eve of the First World War the Pleasure Beach was already making a positive contribution not only to Blackpool's economy, as a visitor attraction, an employer and a powerful contributor to municipal tramway and electricity revenues, but also to its image, as a novel centre for outdoor fun deploying new technologies in ways that were entirely supportive of the town's 'Progress' motto, and as a respectable amusement park which had successfully overcome most of the reservations harboured by middle-class residents, estate agents and nearby shopkeepers.[3]

Blackpool Pleasure Beach soon came to be seen as an emblem of industrial saturnalia, although the phrase itself is a later invention: a place where dignity could be abandoned, fears indulged, conventional restraints set aside and respectability suspended under safe and controlled conditions; but from an early stage, and especially during the 1920s and above all the 1930s, it also became identified with industrial modernity, with a pleasure architecture of and for the intermittently liberated 'masses', with clean lines, streamlined and simplified decorative motifs, whiteness and brightness. It offered a seductive combination of the crazy, the terrifying, the reassuring and the secure; and under Leonard Thompson and Joseph Emberton, especially, it confirmed its separation from the alternative popular seaside of the sideshow and the freak show, of titillation and fraud, of games of chance and fortune telling, that was associated with Blackpool's Golden Mile or Coney Island's Bowery. It parted company completely with the more dirty and disreputable side of the amusement park business, as increasingly identified with those aspects of the Coney Island and other transatlantic amusement parks that horrified the young Walt Disney ('dirty, phony places run by

2 Tony Bennett, 'Hegemony, ideology, pleasure: Blackpool', in T. Bennett, C. Mercer and J. Woollacott (eds.), *Popular Culture and Social Relations* (Milton Keynes, 1986), pp. 147–51; Fred Gray, *Designing the Seaside* (London, 2006), pp. 271–8.

3 Vanessa Toulmin, *Electric Edwardians* (London, 2006); Cross and Walton, *Playful Crowd*, Chapter 2.

**The Pleasure Beach visiting public in the late twentieth century did not live down to the jaundiced views of its most prejudiced critics, but the bare-chested teenagers in the 'Swinging Gyms' on the Watson Road overpass, the scantily clad women and visible response to hot weather would all have been alien to the period between the 1890s and the 1960s, which is often viewed as in some senses a long extension of the Victorian age.**

tough-looking people') and came under increasing pressure from the reforming regime of New York's Commissioner Robert Moses. There were no such pressures or even adverse commentaries directed at the inter-war Pleasure Beach, and this helped it to overcome threats from road realignment and municipal competition to become firmly established as an essential part of Blackpool's leisure menu, as it embraced and profited from the cult of fresh air, sunshine and exercise that came to the fore at the seaside, as elsewhere, in inter-war Britain.[4]

The post-war Pleasure Beach became increasingly important to Blackpool's holiday economy, especially under Geoffrey Thompson in the last quarter of the twentieth century. As the competitive pressures on Blackpool mounted from the early 1970s onwards, and as most of the town's live shows lost their starry performers to film and television, and to more lucrative engagements elsewhere, the Pleasure Beach stood out as

4 Cross and Walton, *Playful Crowd*, Chapter 4 and p. 170.

Blackpool's great innovator, a family firm with a strong identity in an increasingly corporate environment, and with the capacity to generate enormous publicity from spectacular, and spectacularly expensive, new rides, which tended increasingly to emphasize their power to terrify as well as to disorientate and destabilise. In keeping with this change of emphasis, teenagers and young adults, sometimes hunting in packs, were more in evidence from the 1960s onwards, although never to the exclusion of family parties; and despite the occasional panics about football hooligans, and a string of isolated violent incidents (usually in the bars rather than on the amusement park itself), the Pleasure Beach handled the 'evening economy' of binge drinking and 'stag and hen' parties more effectively and inclusively than did the pubs and clubs of central Blackpool. But gentler rides remained in abundance on the crowded site, to cater for most tastes, and the Pleasure Beach's alternative identity as a living commercial museum of the amusement park industry was becoming well established by the 1970s. Like Blackpool as a whole, the Pleasure Beach in the last quarter of the twentieth century lived by a combination of nostalgia, for an industrial way of life and leisure that was now in terminal decline, and the celebration of the modern and the path-breaking on which their prosperities had been founded. Tensions between nostalgia, modernity and the best way to turn a profit were heightening during these years, and were still working themselves out at the beginning of the new millennium.[5] But throughout the later twentieth century the Pleasure Beach's importance to Blackpool's economy grew more obvious, whether as visitor attraction in its own right (as its towering pre-eminence among free-to-enter tourist destinations in Britain became unassailable), as international symbol (rivalling the Tower) of Blackpool's status as premier popular holiday destination, or as one of the town's largest employers, finding niches in the process for both the rootless and for the part-time in need of additional income (the elderly and (semi)-retired, students funding their way through courses, single parents). In this latter guise it played its part in the attraction of migrants to Blackpool's growing 'houses in multiple occupation' sector, with the collapse of the cheaper end of the boarding-house economy, but also offered opportunities to members of those disadvantaged groups within the labour market that bulked disproportionately large in Blackpool's population, as they did in many old-established seaside resorts at the turn of the millennium. There was nothing philanthropic about this, but in meeting its own needs the Pleasure Beach did make its contribution to alleviating the employment

[5] Bennett, 'Hegemony', p. 151; Cross and Walton, *Playful Crowd*, Chapter 6; Walton and Wood, 'World heritage seaside'.

problems that were generated by Blackpool's enduringly seasonal and fluctuating economy.[6]

The Pleasure Beach has come to be firmly identified with Blackpool, as a key attraction that is essential to the town's continuing viability as a popular seaside resort. It is, however, an emblem of Blackpool itself rather than of the British seaside more generally. It originated among the sand dunes, it was vulnerable to flooding as recently as 1977, and its seaside location is inseparable from its allure, but it does not express a distinctively 'seaside' identity in the same way as piers, promenades, Winter Gardens and their associated paraphernalia. Belle Vue and the Crystal Palace, respectively on the fringes of central Manchester and in the outer suburbs of south-west London, were inland amusement parks, with origins in the middle quarters of the nineteenth century, that began life more than half a century or more before the Pleasure Beach, and recruited visitors from wide catchment areas, but failed to sustain their vitality through the twentieth century. Meanwhile the rise of new inland theme parks such as Drayton Manor, founded in 1949 by a member of the Bryan family of slot machine manufacturers and moving strongly into the world of roller coasters and thrill rides from the early 1980s, Thorpe Park and Chessington on the outer fringes of London, and the reinvented Alton Towers of the 1970s and 1980s, might be seen as part of a wider challenge to the dominance of the seaside as a pleasure site and destination in the late twentieth century, but were actually a continuation of established patterns in new forms, often associated with former 'stately homes' (Drayton Manor, Alton Towers) and with a transition during the 1980s from educational aspirations to a concentration on thrill rides (Thorpe Park).[7] Seaside resorts provide a captive market for such attractions, as opposed to the theme park as 'stand alone' destination and object of a special journey, and the seaside location adds an extra dimension to their distinctive identity, but this is not an exclusively seaside phenomenon. Indeed, the demise of most of the other major British seaside amusement parks in the late twentieth and early twenty first century left the Pleasure Beach looking like the odd one out, as both the oldest of the big theme parks and the only one to be at the seaside and to form part of a large urban resort. At this period, the Pleasure Beach itself began to seem almost embarrassed about its seaside location, promoting itself as a stand-alone

6 Walton, *Blackpool*, Chapters 6–7; Walton, *British Seaside*, Chapter 6; Office of the Deputy Prime Minister, Select Committee on Coastal Towns, 2006, written evidence.

7 H. Pussard, '101 places rolled into one', in J.K. Walton (ed.), *Histories of Tourism* (Clevedon, 2005); Cross and Walton, *Playful Crowd*, pp. 209–10; Michael J. Fisher, *Alton Towers: a Gothic Wonderland* (Stafford, 1999); http://www.melright.com/bryans/museum.htm accessed 4 Nov. 2006; www.themeuk.net/Thorpehistory.html accessed 4 Nov. 2006.

destination like Alton Towers, Drayton Manor and Thorpe Park, building the 'Big Blue' hotel so that people could stay 'on resort', and even changing its name to 'Pleasure Beach Blackpool' to reduce the prominence of Blackpool, reflecting the changing balance of image and power between the park and the resort that hosted it. All this should also warn us against the notion that it is necessary to go to the seaside to find the liminal or the carnivalesque, the sense of life 'on the edge' or at the gateway, the suspension of constraints or the embrace of an alternative reality: these things are equally possible, in principle, in the more prosaic surroundings of rural Staffordshire, or even on the urban fringe of a suburbanised market town like Tamworth. What does mark the difference, in the case of the Pleasure Beach, is its close relationship with the rest of Blackpool and the ways in which the resort's distinctively seaside entertainments and ambience complement and infiltrate the experience of the amusement park itself.

The Pleasure Beach, in its own right, is not an obvious or uncomplicated symbol of the British seaside. Where does it stand in relation to ideas about British or English identity, or to ideas about regional identities within Britain? In terms of visitor catchment area and external visibility, it followed Blackpool's trajectory in moving from a regional and predominantly industrial working-class (or 'popular') profile in the early twentieth century to a more up-market, national, family-oriented mix between the 1920s and the 1960s. As an alternative popular entertainment capital to London during this period, Blackpool became identified with celebrations of northern identity that emphasized the 'work hard, play hard' ethic of straight-talking, wealth-creating northern industrial society, set against notions of the effete, ungrounded imagined 'south' and especially the metropolis.[8] By the late twentieth century matters were becoming more complicated, and the Pleasure Beach under Geoffrey Thompson embraced and catered for a new generation looking for more intense and challenging thrills and sensations, while at the same time striving to remain family friendly and to maintain traditions of security and respectability. This was entirely compatible with reaching out to new markets among 'British Asians' and seeking international patronage, and it did not exclude the 'pink pound' alongside the stag and hen parties and the student seekers after kitsch excitement; but it did not entail carving out a separate identity within Blackpool's engagement with changing ideas about what it was to be British, and indeed Irish.[9]

8 Bennett, 'Hegemony', pp. 144–6; Joyce, *Visions of the People*, pp. 165–71.

9 J.K. Walton, 'Blackpool and the varieties of Britishness', in S. Caunce et al. (eds.), *Relocating Britishness* (Manchester, 2004), pp. 53–70.

The Pleasure Beach's own claim to a distinctive place in Blackpool's changing relationship with Englishness and Britishness lies in its relationship with the United States, and with arguments about the Americanisation of British popular culture. From its earliest days the Pleasure Beach took pride in importing the latest in American amusement machinery for the delectation of its crowds of pleasure-seekers; and the transfer of technology across the Atlantic, familiar from the Lancashire cotton industry, persisted long after the latter's demise, although by the late 1930s European fairground influences were coming in alongside the American, while British technology was always part of the picture alongside the imports.[10] This was not a matter of American practices imposing themselves and transforming this aspect of British popular culture from without, although fears about this possibility, and about Blackpool as a gateway for the diffusion of Americanisation, were widely expressed in the 1930s, not least by J.B. Priestley in his influential *English Journey*.[11] It was more a question of British entrepreneurs taking from an American menu of amusement devices whatever they thought to be a likely paying proposition in Blackpool, adapting it where necessary to local tastes, evaluating the results and reacting accordingly. The Pleasure Beach was not an Irish Sea outpost of Coney Island or Kennywood. It was a hybrid between American and British practices and preferences, nourished by transatlantic friendships between the Thompson family and their American suppliers and collaborators; but it took its atmosphere and ambience from the Blackpool holiday crowds, rather than trying to impose anything alien on them. The continuing success of the Pleasure Beach while Coney Island went into seemingly terminal decline, together with the recurrent puzzlement and culture shock of American visitors encountering the Blackpool amusement park for the first time, lend strong support to this argument.[12]

The relationship between the Pleasure Beach and the Disney theme parks, as the latter developed over the second half of the twentieth century, also bears examination as an extension of this agenda. In some respects the Leonard Thompson and Joseph Emberton project of the 1930s to construct a clean, safe, modern, family-friendly amusement park might look like an

[10] D.J. Jeremy, 'The international diffusion of cotton manufacturing technology, 1750–1990s', in D. Farnie and D.J. Jeremy (eds.), *The Fibre that Changed the World* (Oxford, 2004).

[11] J.K. Walton, 'The transatlantic seaside: Blackpool and Coney Island', in N. Campbell, J. Davies and G. McKay (eds.), *Issues in Americanisation and Culture* (Edinburgh, 2004), pp. 111–25.

[12] Cross and Walton, *Playful Crowd*, Chapter 4.

anticipation of Disney, and a Disney delegation visited the faded Pleasure Beach of the post-war austerity years as part of the research for planning Disneyland. There were two crucial differences. In the first place, the Pleasure Beach, like Blackpool itself, lacked a 'master narrative' to pull the holiday experience together; and the rides themselves were experiences in their own right, without trying to draw customers into extended fantasies or versions of magical stories that invited the suspension of disbelief and the acceptance of a parallel universe of fairytale and nostalgia. The Pleasure Beach had no equivalent of Disney's zones or 'lands', nor did it have a reservoir of characters, film plots and other allusions on which to draw for fantasy and promotional purposes. Each ride had its own identity without pretensions to forming part of an 'imagineered' whole. Nor did it present an imagined past, or an imagined geography, as if it were a real set of experiences. It drew upon evocative images of imagined places and experiences, from gold mine and river caves to Viking legend; but the fantasies were isolated from each other and always subordinated to the physical experience of the ride. The Pleasure Beach, in contrast with Disney, was more fairground than theme park.[13] Secondly, the Pleasure Beach appealed to a different set of visiting publics, and the contrast was more than just an international one. The Disney enterprises aimed at a middle-class market drawn from the whole of the United States, and then beyond: a car culture whose consumption levels and aspirations were far beyond anything the British economy could offer, even as levels of popular affluence rose from the 1950s onwards. The Pleasure Beach's core market remained rooted in the working classes of northern and midland England and southern Scotland, even as the industries that sustained it and the communities that nurtured it were coming under increasing and sometimes intolerable pressures in the closing decades of the twentieth century. Moreover, the Pleasure Beach's location was becoming increasingly unfashionable, as the geography of economic dynamism, wealth, consumer power, fashion and holidaymaking shifted inexorably southwards, to London, parts of the south coast and of south-west England, Normandy, Brittany and the Mediterranean. The Pleasure Beach still aspired to modernity, but it was surrounded by the debris of the industrial civilisation which had given it birth. Coney Island, Atlantic City and the New Jersey shore had similar problems in the United States; but Disney catered for the snowbirds and long-range vacationers of a much more prosperous consumer society, which idealised the nuclear family, created child-centred consumerism and needed a different kind of escape. What is revealing about this comparison

[13] Bennett, 'Hegemony', pp. 151–2.

is the extent and nature of the contrasts.[14] In many ways, indeed, Geoffrey Thompson's Pleasure Beach of the last quarter of the twentieth century came to have more in common with Beamish and some of the other open-air industrial museums that proliferated alongside the new theme parks during the Thatcher years, than with Disneyland or Disneyworld, which after all never found a home in Britain.[15] But what it was about, above all, was escapist fun and, increasingly, the public enjoyment of thrills and fear. This is a world away from Disney, although aspects of the Disney menu have been moving in these directions in recent years, and it is much closer to many other American leisure experiences.

Blackpool Pleasure Beach is a national and international phenomenon. It demands appraisal on those terms, comparatively and in terms of assessment of its influence on other places and other cultures. But it remains a product of its time and place, and of the historical processes that have shaped its development, although it has done some shaping of its own in return. It is unique, and remarkable; and its roots lie in the first Industrial Revolution of its Lancashire hinterland, which gave so much to the world, for better and worse, from association football in its professional form to the Co-operative movement and the popular seaside holiday.[16] It has adapted better to the post-industrial (and post-imperial) world than less rooted rivals, and it remains in the hands of its founding family (another legacy of early industrial culture) after overcoming a series of succession crises.[17] Its unique position among British amusement parks has been highlighted all the more by the disappearance of so many rivals, as opportunities for profit from housing and commericial redevelopment have been seductive enough to produce a long roll-call of recent, current and impending closures since the turn of the millennium, from Spanish City at Whitley Bay to Coney Beach at Porthcawl and Merlin's at St Ives, and including evocative venues like Margate's Dreamland. The Pleasure Beach's future, like that of Blackpool as a whole, is at a crossroads; but this book has shown how much it is possible to learn from its past.

14 Ibid., 146, 152; Gary Cross, *An All-Consuming Century* (New York, 2000); Gary Cross, *The Cute and the Cool* (Oxford, 2004).

15 Cross and Walton, *Playful Crowd*, Chapters 5–6.

16 Walton, *Lancashire*, Chapter 13.

17 Mary B. Rose, *Firms, Networks and Business Values: the British and American Cotton Industries since 1750* (Cambridge, 2000).

# Index